Intentional Parenting

His Word; Our actions; Eternal rewards

Tricia Simmons

Copyright © 2008 by Tricia Simmons

Intentional Parenting
His Word; Our actions; Eternal rewards
by Tricia Simmons

Printed in the United States of America

ISBN 978-1-60477-945-5

All rights reserved solely by the author. The author guarantees all contents are original and do not infringe upon the legal rights of any other person or work. No part of this book may be reproduced in any form without the permission of the author. The views expressed in this book are not necessarily those of the publisher.

Unless otherwise indicated, Bible quotations are taken from The King James Version, and The Holy Bible, New Living Translation, Copyright © 1996, 2004, Used by permission of Tyndale House Publishers, Inc., Wheaton, Illinois 60189, and The New King James Version, Copyright © 1982 by Thomas Nelson, Inc., Used by permission.

www.xulonpress.com

Acknowledgements

My heart overflows with thanks to my Lord for allowing me to be an instrument in His hands. To Him be all the glory for any families that are helped by the words in this book!

To Stephen, my beloved, I give my love and thanks for encouraging me and supporting me through all the stages of birthing this book. I would have to write another book to express all the ways you helped bring this one to fruition. Your life is a testament that intentional parenting works.

My sweet girls, Saige and Haley, you were so understanding of my need to "focus" on writing. Being your mommy has inspired me and blessed me in profound ways.

To my parents and siblings who helped me grow up to believe I had the ability to do great things, thank you. What you spoke into me is proof that there is power in our words. All those little notes I wrote to you all the time must have been preparation for a time such as this.

Debby, Melanie, Diana, Jessica, and Kay, I am blessed to call you my friends. Your excitement for me to complete this has been precious to me. Thanks for not tiring of hearing about it.

Diane, your editing skills were put to good use, for a good purpose. I am indebted to you.

Table of Contents

Introduction ix

Chapter 1   Train up a Child 11

Chapter 2   Teach Them Diligently 21

Chapter 3   Become as a Child 33

Chapter 4   Lay Aside Every Weight 41

Chapter 5   I Formed Thee 49

Chapter 6   The Word Equips 59

Chapter 7   A Child of God From the Womb 67

Chapter 8   Walk as Thy Father Walked 79

Chapter 9	Discipline 91

Chapter 10	Lost and Found........................103

Introduction

Intentional parenting is deciding to do what it takes to train up your child in the Way they should go. This means having a goal and a plan of action *before* you face each new challenge your child brings. Anyone can parent by accident— reacting to behaviors and situations as they arise, but it takes determination and commitment to parent *intentionally*.

Many resources are available today to aid parents in their pursuit of child-rearing; however, the most valuable resource often overlooked is the Bible. To be an intentional parent, you must first learn God's Word and apply it daily to your own life. Everything we need to know, even parenting, is there to guide us if we just look. Important commands and lessons are waiting to be gleaned from God's Word. I would like to take you to some of those scriptures, and I also encourage you to seek more out for yourself. Once you have a foundation of Truth you will be better prepared to handle the situations that arise with each stage of development.

My hope is that through this book, you are encouraged to be the intentional parent God wants you to be and your child needs you to be.

Chapter 1

Train up a Child
Proverbs 22:6

Train up a child in the way he should go: and when he is old, he will not depart from it.

Wow! What a promise! If I train up my child everything will turn out right. Right? Let's take a look at why this scripture is important and why as parents we must obey this principle in order for the promise to be true.

Proverbs 22:6 tells us to, "Train up a child in the way he should go." But how? How do we accomplish this? First we must understand what the "way" is that they should go. We know from John 14:6 that Jesus is "the way the truth and the life" therefore we know the *way* our children should go is Jesus! Our children must be taught of His ways, walk in His ways, and love His ways. But how do we *train* them in the *way?* We make Jesus the center of their life!

Intentional Parenting

I have some beautiful vines planted in my yard that require a trellis to twine themselves around. I have to go out periodically and make sure that the new growth is being trained to cling to the trellis. If I wait too long to do this, it begins hanging down and becomes entangled in the other bushes growing nearby. But if I keep the trellis at its center, as its support for growth, it grows upward able to show off its beauty. In this same fashion we must train up our children to cling to Jesus as a vine clings to a trellis, so they will grow and flourish, bearing the fruit they were created to produce. If we don't give them Jesus to cling to they will seek out the other things around them and become ensnared in the "yoke of bondage" spoken of in Galatians 5:1. Our children need to be given the proper support to enable them to grow in the correct *way* so that when they are old they will not depart from it.

As parents we hope, we pray, we believe that our children will naturally be *vines* that will *cling* only to the proper support provided. We see their future growing into the beautiful flowering vine we want them to become. Children are much like a vine in that they can be trained to cling to Jesus; however, it doesn't come naturally. In fact, like some vines, they need to be tied or guided to its support and even then, as it grows, its stems may pull away. If we can begin when they are young, it gives them time to learn Jesus is who they should reach for and cling to.

While training your child to cling to what is good you will inevitably find them unruly at times, fighting or questioning your authority. Usually this indicates that pruning is needed. Pruning can be difficult as the stems are sometimes thorny and hard to handle, or are in hard to reach places. But if we don't make the effort to do the hard things, it won't bear the fruit it was created to bear; instead, it just keeps growing and producing more stems not ever fulfilling the beauty God intended it to have. Vines must be pruned regularly to encourage new growth and flowers. It's hard sometimes to prune a lovely, green, growing bush and it's not easy to take things away from our children when they think it's something they must have; nevertheless, if it's keeping them from growing properly a good pruning will allow them to flourish and bear good fruit. A vine that has been properly *trained* and pruned grows into the tall, thriving, fragrant creation God intended it to be. Just as the vine creates a beautiful fragrance that the breeze can catch and carry on the wind to be enjoyed by all those nearby, God wants our children to grow up to be a sweet perfume spreading the knowledge of Christ everywhere (2 Corinthians 2:14-16).

As our children grow older they will encounter more temptations and have more opportunities to become entangled in things around them. This is why it is so important to be aware of what your child is surrounded by. Even when we are *tied* to Jesus our hands and feet can still reach out to things that are not beneficial. Who are your child's friends? Do you know what they are like? Are they good influences? "Birds of a feather flock together." By knowing who is surrounding your child you can help protect and

Intentional Parenting

---

guide them away from those who would pressure them to do wrong.

As parents we like to think that our child is strong enough to stand up to peer-pressure. Some kids are indeed better at saying no to what is not right; but many find this difficult and the desire to please their friends or fit in overrides their desire to do the right thing. One way to help a child be strong is to consistently speak to them their worth in your eyes and God's. They have to believe that if they stand up for what is right and by doing so a friend turns on them, then perhaps that person was not a true friend. They must know that you and God will never forsake them (Hebrews 13:5). It is important for our children to understand they need to please God in their words and actions, not their peers. If they are trying to please people that are not nice to them, thinking that if they act like them or do things for them, then they'll receive their approval, then your child is in danger. Conforming to those around us to be accepted is a common thing. It's natural for us to want to be accepted and included. Especially when we think, "They are better than I am." Feeling inferior can drive even the most well behaved person to make bad choices because they want approval. Again, they need to comprehend their worth in God's eyes, and this is something that takes constant reinforcement from you and prayer that God will help them. Our children's worth cannot be based upon others approval, it must be tied to Jesus. When your child shares concerns about a friend that is making bad choices, lead them in prayer for that friend; and be there to comfort your child if they feel

Intentional Parenting

they need to distance them self from that relationship. This is all part of training them how to handle the difficulties of life and conform to His image, not this world's (Romans 8:29, 12:2). Be aware of signs that your child is becoming entangled in things that could harm them. Is their speech changing? Are they becoming disrespectful? Are they becoming increasingly disobedient? What could be influencing them? Could it be their friends? Sometimes it's as simple as a book, TV show, or a computer game.

I remember a time when my daughter was behaving in a way that was unlike her. I had been wondering what was going on, when one day I was watching a certain TV show with her and realized she was imitating the young girl on the program. Now mind you I am very selective of what programs my daughters watch and thought this to be an innocent program. There is no sexual activity, bad language, or violent content. It is a show about a loving family; however, this one character, who elicited a lot of laughs on the show, was thought "cute" because, though she was very young, she would say things that were *big*. As an adult, I can watch something like this and it won't affect me, but my little girl, who likes to make people laugh and be cute, thought that by being like this girl on the show she, too, would be cute. Well, it was anything but cute! In fact I told my daughter this character was actually behaving quite rudely and disrespectfully. My daughter admitted she was behaving like this character and agreed that, for a time, she didn't need to watch it. It's amazing the difference it makes when we look at things through a child's eyes. I'm happy to report that the unbecoming conduct stopped after this enlightenment. Because she is being tied to Jesus she was able to see the difference between the behavior she should have versus the behavior of this character. I would have had no basis, no foundation to strengthen my position, without the support of the Way.

We must also make a point to recognize when our children are making good choices; and praise them when we see them striving to cling to Jesus. Telling them Jesus is proud of them, and so is Daddy and Mommy, means the world to them. When they make good choices on their own, because it is the right thing to do, it needs to be noticed and rewarded. It is important for us to acknowledge and bless them for being obedient to our training. No matter the age of your vine, in addition to the necessary pruning, regular fertilization is also vital to its health.

Our words have an enormous impact on our children and we need to be careful what we speak not only to them, but in their hearing. James 3:10 states, "Out of the same mouth proceedeth blessing and cursing. My brethren, these things ought not so to be." There is the power in our words to bless or curse our children. You may think, "I would never curse my child!" Yet, when they are standing beside you and you tell someone that your child is messy, fearful, shy, stupid, fat, lazy, etc. you are labeling that child with a "curse." They may struggle with some things, but that doesn't meant they should be cursed with a label that identifies them with that struggle. Just because a child becomes fearful during a storm

Intentional Parenting

does not make them afraid of everything. Be careful to not speak curses.

Parents, please consider that many of the behaviors our children have are because we either model it to them or we speak it into them. When we take our children to a new place they may feel apprehensive; it does not edify them to say, "You may not like this." That is just setting them up for a bad experience. I remember overhearing a mother, with her child standing beside her, tell her child's Sunday school teachers, "He will probably cry when I leave." Well, what do you think happened when she left? He cried! The teachers were able to console him and all was well, but I couldn't help but wonder if he would have cried if she hadn't said anything negative. I wondered if she had said he was excited about Sunday school and was going to have a great time, if he would have even noticed she had gone. If we don't like spiders and we freak out whenever we see one it teaches our children that spiders are something to fear. Now, don't get me wrong, I am one of those people who feel like freaking out if a spider is near me. Little ones I can handle, but anything larger than a centimeter causes me to feel squirmy. Before I became a mom I didn't hesitate to let out a squeal if one came too close; since having children, I have made it a point to act as nonchalant as possible. I will say that while my girls don't really care for spiders I am thankful that at least they don't have a melt down when they see one. When they let me know about one that has gotten too close to them I have made it a point to say, "Oh, it's just a spider, remember you are a million times bigger and it's scared of you!" Okay, maybe my girls aren't a million times bigger, but they get the point. Try not to speak negative (curses) things into your child's life. Instead, shower them with words (blessings) that will edify them and minister grace.

Stop for a moment and ask yourself, "Am I speaking things into my child that will edify them or tear them down?" Ephesians 4:29 tells us, "Let no corrupt communication proceed out of your mouth, but that which is good to the use of edifying, that it may minister grace unto the hearers." If we tell our children they are just like someone that is lazy, mean, selfish, etc. are you edifying them, or tearing them down? Sure our children may act out in a bad way sometimes, but don't make the mistake of telling them they are bad. We have to be very clear when expressing our displeasures with certain behaviors that it is the behavior that is bad, not them. In fact, make it a point to tell them how much you love them and that they are still your wonderful child. This will help them not to think of themselves as "bad," but rather the conduct.

My husband has established a powerful tradition in our home. Each Father's Day he performs a blessing ceremony. This consists of calling our girls to his side, and beginning with the eldest, he prays a blessing over them. We find in Genesis 49 the account of Jacob blessing each of his 12 sons. Jacob speaks into each one of them a very personal blessing for them and their descendants. I can tell you when my husband and girls are sitting there, holding hands with heads bowed, and he speaks blessings into them, there is much tears and love flowing not only from daddy to daughter, but from the Lord toward them both. What an amazing way to celebrate Father's Day!

Parent, it is up to you, with the help of God's Spirit and through His Word, to see that your vine, your child from God, grows in the right way, the Way of Jesus. Our goal as parents should be that as our children grow into adults they bear the fruit that God's Word tells us are love, joy, peace, patience, kindness, goodness, faithfulness, gentleness, and self-control (Galatians 5:22-23 NLT). The best way to achieve this is to be intentional and model for them the Way. We must do this out of obedience to His Word, and trust Him to take care of our vines when they are old.

In the following chapters we will see the instructions our Lord has given us, the intentional parent, for building a trellis of support to accomplish training our children in the Way they should go.

Prayer: Thank you Father for the promise you have given me as a parent. Help me to be intentional in how I parent, so I can train up _____ your Way, that when they're old they would not depart from you. Show me anything in my life, as well as my child's, that may need to be pruned in order for us to be healthy and bear fruit. Help me to be careful of the words I speak, that they would be for Your glory and purpose. I ask this in Jesus name, Amen.

Chapter 2

Teach Them Diligently
Deuteronomy 6:4-7

Hear, O Israel: The LORD our God is one LORD: And thou shalt love the LORD thy God with all thine heart, and with all thy soul, and with all thy might. And these words, which I command thee this day, shall be in thine heart: And thou shalt teach them diligently unto thy children, and shalt talk of them when thou sittest in thine house, and when thou walkest by the way, and when thou liest down, and when thou risest up.

Several years ago after becoming a mother, God began speaking to my heart the importance of children to His Kingdom. God exhorts every parent to teach their children His laws from sun up to sun down. Yet how many parents mention God at all in any given day? I believe many of our problems today would be resolved if parents simply understood it is imperative to train their children to love the Lord with all their heart, soul, mind, and strength beginning at birth and continuing every day thereafter.

As parents, we must take special care to obey the instructions in verse 7. Notice we are to teach God's Word to our children throughout the day and wherever we go! In order to accomplish this effectively you need to be with your child as much as possible. It's not just quality time together, it is quantity if you are going to be intentional in training your child. We must also note that His Word is to be taught diligently, or as one dictionary defines, "showing persistent and hard-working effort." Yes, training our children takes determined, conscientious effort!

It is in our fallen nature to sin, and if our children are not taught daily to choose good over evil and what pleases God over what pleases themselves, there is not much hope for them to suddenly turn from evil when they are teenagers or adults. The Barna Research Group found the probability of someone embracing Jesus as his or her Savior was 32% for those between the ages of 5 and 12 and drops to a mere 4% for those in the 13-18-age range. You see if the pretty packaging satan uses is not removed when they are young then they will believe the lie satan has given them, and the Truth is harder to accept as they grow older. The Truth ends up looking dull and boring because they are seeing through distorted vision. Our children have to be taught there is hope everlasting in a life lived for God and eternal torment for a life served unto themselves and this world.

To make this commitment to daily teach your children it takes an understanding that God created your child and entrusted them to you. God has a plan and a purpose for your child's life, and if you don't teach them to love the Lord their God with all their heart, soul, mind, and strength, who will? The world sure won't! The world will fill their mind with so many lies that they can't even see the Truth. This world is satan's realm, and he is not going to see to it that your child lives a righteous life for God. Satan is out to steal, kill, and destroy (John 10:10) and he wants your child.

> O my people, listen to my instructions. Open your ears to what I am saying, for I will speak to you in a parable. I will teach you hidden lessons from our past—stories we have heard and known, stories our ancestors handed down to us. We will not hide these truths from our children; we will tell the next generation about the glorious deeds of the Lord, about his power and his mighty wonders. For he issued his laws to Jacob; he gave his instructions to Israel. He commanded our ancestors to teach them to their children, so the next generation might know them— even the children not yet born—and they in turn will teach their own children. So each generation should set its hope anew on God, not forgetting his glorious miracles and obeying his commands. Then they will not be like their ancestors—stubborn, rebellious, and unfaithful, refusing

to give their hearts to God. Psalm 78:1-8 (NLT)

There has been a lot of talk in recent years about the state of savings in the U.S. It is said that the current rate of savings is at the lowest rate since the Great Depression. During the Great Depression, millions of people were without jobs so this is understandable; today it's because we spend too much. I am not about to try to give an economics lesson; I simply want to address something that has taken place from a family perspective. The "generation" forgot. Following the Great Depression, when everyone was working again, they made sure to save so that if lean times returned they would be prepared. They worked hard, saved money, bought homes, and had children. These children grew up hearing the stories of what it was like living during the Great Depression. Even if their parents weren't affected as badly as others they still witnessed the devastating effects, and it made such an impression — they remembered it. Then they passed away, and their children reaped their wise parents' decisions to save. Perhaps they inherited a modest home, a family business, or cash. They were blessed. In this blessing they forgot. They had learned from their parents the importance of saving and living modestly so they practiced this way of saving and frugality. But they forgot what their parents had gone through to learn this valuable lesson and so forgot to teach their children. By not sharing the testimony of the former generation the next generation simply enjoyed the fruits of all these blessings and the enjoyment of purchasing power without any of the restraint. We can see today that as we have moved further away from the Great Depression the savings rate has declined. "After that generation died, another generation grew up who did not acknowledge the Lord or remember the mighty things he had done for Israel" (Judges 2:10 NLT).

Just as in the time of the Judges, we too have forgotten to teach the lessons we have learned from the Lord. We face difficulties and we cry out to God just as the children of Israel did in Egypt; He hears our cries and graciously delivers us. We thank him for his mercy, and if we forget to write it down and share it with our children, we forget who He is and what He did for us. We forget that just as He saved us the last time, He'll save us this time. We begin to worry and fret. Yet if we would just remember to hide His Word in our hearts and teach it diligently to our children we have this promise, "If you listen to these regulations and faithfully obey them, the Lord your God will keep his covenant of unfailing love with you, as he promised with an oath to your ancestors. He will love you and bless you, and he will give you many children" (Deuteronomy 7:12 NLT). We have a promise that the Lord will love us, bless us, and give us children; all by simply obeying his Word and remembering to teach our children where He brought us from.

In Deuteronomy 6:12 we are given a warning, "beware lest thou forget the LORD, which brought thee forth out of the land of Egypt, from the house of bondage." There is danger in forgetting the Lord. If we don't teach our children diligently to love the Lord we forget what the Lord has brought us from. We forget that He is worthy of all our praise. We forget that He delivered us from bondage, the bondage of sin. When we forget where He has brought us from we begin to think we have gotten where we are by our own strength. We have to remember God blesses us by His grace because He loves us and wants us to glorify Him.

The Lord understands there is amazing power in a personal experience! In Mark 5:19-20 NLT, we read of Jesus telling the man who he delivered from the legion of demons to "'go home to your family, and tell them everything the Lord has done for you and how merciful he has been.' So the man started off to visit the Ten Towns of that region and began to proclaim the great things Jesus had done for him; and everyone was amazed at what he told them." There is power in remembering and sharing where we have come from. When we share these faith building experiences it helps us to pass on that legacy. People are amazed when they have known you and see the evidence of all the Lord has done for you. This same personal experience speaks strongly to your children, too. Even if you were privileged to grow up knowing and serving the Lord, this is a testimony to your faith. Your witness shows the world we don't have to conform to its image. When we forget what the Lord has done for us, when we fail to share our story, we become susceptible to sin. When we follow the command in Deuteronomy 6:4-7, God will be the center of our life. It would be hard to break a commandment if you have just finished telling your child how God saved you. It would be hard not to love your neighbor as yourself if you speak of God's love and mercy throughout the day.

Now, you may be thinking "How do I do this?" Surround yourself with God. Don't forget Him as you live your life day by day. What do you have on your desk at work? Most people have a calendar. How about one with beautiful pictures and a Psalm? How about a screen saver with your favorite scripture, or a picture of your family along with that scripture? You could have a devotional that you keep at work for your break time or lunch. A devotional doesn't have to be an hour long; there are many that take only 10 minutes. The point is you are remembering the Lord. I know people who keep the Bible on compact disc in the car and listen to it on the way to work. Anything you can do to remember who you serve will help you when life throws you a temptation. In the same way that this helps you, it will help your child.

The best time to begin diligently teaching your child is before they even enter this world. Pray for your baby while still in the womb that they would be all that God has created them to be. Pray for yourself and your spouse that you would be the parents your child needs you to be. Pray for God's wisdom to parent according to His Word in every situation. Then after they are born continue praying for them while you feed or rock them to sleep. Play music that glorifies God and sing songs that tell of God's goodness. As they grow older give them a children's Bible to read together each night to teach them God's Word

Intentional Parenting

and how special it is to us. Pray as a family at bedtime and give thanks together before each meal. When old enough to read independently provide them a devotional they can do at the same time you are doing yours. Be a family that can say "as for me and my house, we will serve the Lord" (Joshua 24:15). The best way to teach is always by example. No matter the age, don't just tell your children to love the Lord, show them! Do service projects together. Serve together at a soup kitchen or maybe some secret service projects; such as bringing up your neighbors trash can from the road so they don't have to. If your children are older you could, as a family, pitch in to help with your church's Vacation Bible School or go on a mission trip. The possibilities are endless.

You may have noticed I gave several examples involving prayer. This is because we are told in 1 Thessalonians 5:17, "Pray without ceasing." Our children must be taught how to fellowship with the Lord. He desires us to talk to him as a friend. He desires us to take our ideas, our concerns, our wants, and needs to Him anytime, anywhere. I entered a search into my Bible software for the number of times it said "prayed" because I wanted to see how many instances there are of people praying in scripture. I saw scores of beautiful examples God has given us in His Word of how He listens and responds to the prayers of His people. Never underestimate the power of your prayers as a parent or the power of your child's prayers. As your child grows older it will be very important for him or her to know they can talk to God as a friend. There will be things that come their way that they can't talk to anyone else about; but if they know they have a friend in Jesus, the God who created them and loves them, and they have been trained to talk to Him everyday about everything, they will know they can go to Him in prayer. "Don't worry about anything; instead, pray about everything. Tell God what you need, and thank him for all he has done" (Philippians 4:6 NLT). By weaving prayer daily into your diligent training, it will come naturally to your child to take everything to the Lord in prayer.

Please don't read this and be discouraged if you have not been an intentional parent since the birth of your children. It is never too late to begin. It is never too late to teach your children of God's ways. Instead of living in regret of what you wish you had done; be honest with your children about your mistakes. Use this as a testimony of God's love for you and your child, that He would make a point to open your eyes to the importance of living a life unto Him. Use this as an opportunity to say to your child, "I have sinned by not following God's commands as a parent, as He has forgiven me, will you?" Then rise up and be the parent God wants you to be. It is not always easy going against all that the world throws at our families, but with God's help and His wisdom that you are praying for, you can do it!

Tips to help:

- Begin your day together in prayer and in His Word. This doesn't have to be a lengthy time

commitment; the focus is more about the good habits you are teaching.
- Have children's Bible songs they can listen and sing along with at home or in the car.
- Speaking of the car, after graduating from the "Wee Sing Bible Songs" we began listening to Focus on the Family's Adventures in Odyssey series. As a family, we love these stories! (They have blessed my husband and me as much as our girls!)
- Car time is also a great time to visit with our children about what's going on in their lives. Use this time to connect with them.
- Some time ago we began a new way to give thanks for our meals. As we all hold hands one of us begins with, "Thank you Jesus for this day", the next says, "and this food" the next, "and your many blessings." The last says "Bless this food to the nourishment and strength of our bodies" and all together we say, "In Jesus name, Amen!" Of course you can adapt this to the size of your family and what you like to say. Our girls have enjoyed implementing this and it's teaching the good habit of giving thanks. (And yes, we practice this at restaurants as well.)
- If you spend time outdoors with your children it's easy to teach them about the Lord. You can point to anything in nature and teach them of God's awesome creativity. If your children can see God in the beauty of nature they will always be reminded of Him.

Intentional Parenting

- Some of our best "heart-to-hearts" have been at bed time. No matter the age of your child, there is something about being tucked in the safety of their bed and in semi-darkness which helps them to open up and share their hopes and fears. I have had 9:00 bedtimes turn into 11:00 because I was not about to stop the flow between our hearts. Be willing to stop and listen when they begin to tell you about their day. Stop and take the time to share things you went through as a child so they know you really do understand. You will never regret spending this time with your child; the benefits are priceless!

Prayer: Thank you Father for your example. You are always available to us, anytime, anywhere, ready to teach us and help us in our life. Help me be an example of this to my children. Help me remember to slow down and listen to my child's needs and use those teachable moments throughout the day to show them your way. Help me to remember where you have brought me from and to teach my children the mighty things you've done. In Jesus name I pray, Amen.

Chapter 3

Become as a Child
Matthew 18:3

Except ye be converted, and become as little children, ye shall not enter into the kingdom of heaven.

Parents, as adults we tend to underestimate the ability of children to learn and understand the Lord. Jesus said, "Except ye be converted, and become as little children, ye shall not enter into the kingdom of heaven." He was referring to their simple, pure, trusting faith. This is reflected in the statistic given in the previous chapter. The likelihood of someone over 12 coming to believe in Jesus drops dramatically because their child faith is being destroyed by the influences surrounding them. Remember, if they are not trained to cling to Jesus and pruned when needed then they are more likely to get ensnared in the things of this world. He desires us all to be as children looking to Him for all our needs. Placing our hand in the hand of the Father and allowing Him to lead us on life's journey, takes faith. He desires us to trust Him to "supply all your need according to his riches in glory by Christ Jesus," (Philippians 4:19). Children instinctively know how to do this. So, this is why He said, we must become as children to enter the kingdom of heaven. They know they can depend upon their parents to love them, feed them, clothe them, and give them shelter. Are you becoming as a child and trusting in your Heavenly Father for all your needs? Are you modeling for your child a pure, trusting faith in Jesus?

There is a simple song sung in many Sunday school classes that you may well know. "Oh be careful little eyes what you see, oh be careful little eyes what you see, for the Father up above is looking down in love, oh be careful little eyes what you see." Then it goes on to include ears what you hear, mouths what you say, and feet where you go. If children have to be careful of these things so do we! Where does the Bible teach us that at the age of eighteen or at any age we are suddenly exempt from refraining from sin? It doesn't. It says, "Except ye be converted, and become as little children, ye shall not enter into the kingdom of heaven." Think about that, become as children. Do you allow your child to see nudity? Then why, as God's child would you watch it? Do you allow your child to attend R-rated movies where their eyes and ears receive things contrary to Christ? Why not let them? It's not good for them you say?

Why then is it okay for you? At what age is it ever okay to do these things?

You see, it all begins when we are young and are not taught that "whatsoever ye do, do all to the glory of God" (1 Corinthians 10:31). If you were not brought up to believe that there are things inherently wrong no matter the age, then there is not a problem doing them when you become an adult. And if there is not really anything wrong with adults doing them then it's easier to allow our children to watch movies that have "just a few bad words." It will also be okay for them to read a book that desensitizes them toward the occult. It's no big deal to let them listen to that song or allow our daughters to dance provocatively when they're only six since they don't understand what they're mimicking! You see, if you have not become as a child, how can you teach them to stay pure as a child?

> Unto the pure all things are pure: but unto them that are defiled and unbelieving is nothing pure; but even their mind and conscience is defiled. They profess that they know God; but in works they deny him, being abominable, and disobedient, and unto every good work reprobate. Titus 1:15-16

> There is a generation that curseth their father, and doth not bless their mother. There is a generation that are pure in their own eyes, and yet is not washed from their filthiness. Proverbs 30: 11-12

Let's take a look at purity. Proverbs 20:11 says, "Even a child is known by his doings, whether his work be pure, and whether it be right." What are your child's *doings* saying? As an adult, yet still God's child, what are *your doings* saying? Are they pure and right?

> Finally, brethren, whatsoever things are true, whatsoever things are honest, whatsoever things are just, whatsoever things are pure, whatsoever things are lovely, whatsoever things are of good report; if there be any virtue, and if there be any praise, think on these things. Philippians 4:8

"...whatsoever things are pure...think on these things." Are you keeping your child's surroundings pure? Are you giving them pure things to hold on to so they can grow up in His way? Are their eyes and ears receiving pure things to think on? Or, are they reaching out and holding on to the impure things of this world because it's all they have? "Blessed are the pure in heart: for they shall see God" (Matthew 5:8).

There is a popular movement occurring in many youth groups today, and that is a Purity Pledge marked by receiving a Purity Ring. The pledge is a promise to stay sexually pure until marriage. I think in theory this is a wonderful tool to encourage children and give them a support base that is lacking in our secular society. The concern I have with this pledge is it doesn't go far enough in teaching children or their parents what purity means. There are many teens who think as long as they don't have sexual intercourse they are still pure. They may be "virgins," but they are not remaining pure if they are doing everything but having sexual intercourse. Purity goes beyond sexual purity; it is about being pure in heart.

> If you keep yourself pure, you will be a special utensil for honorable use. Your life will be clean, and you will be ready for the Master to use you for every good work. Run from anything that stimulates youthful lusts. Instead, pursue righteous living, faithfulness, love, and peace. Enjoy the companionship of those who call on the Lord with pure hearts.
> 2 Timothy 2:21-22 NLT

We see from scripture purity should be something we strive for in every area of our life. It won't help your child to take a purity pledge if they are allowed to listen to impure music that boasts of sexual triumphs. A purity pledge won't do a lot of good if your child's eyes are allowed to be filled with visions of sexual immorality. A purity pledge will be hard to keep if they look at themselves as something to stimulate lust and not a vessel for honorable use. Help your child flee from youthful lust by placing well-marked boundaries in their life. It is hard today to protect our children from the onslaught of impurity. It's on TV, at the grocery store check out stand, on billboards, and the internet. You may not be able to control all the outside influences; however, you can control what is allowed to enter your home and who they hang out with. Remember, the Father up above is looking down in love and that is if you are a child, teen, or adult. Help them stay as a child, pure and innocent, in the Way.

Parent, if *you* have become as a child, then you will be able to help your child walk in the way of Jesus. Repentance is a perfect example of becoming as a child. As adults we are often too proud to admit we are not perfect. We don't want others to judge us or maybe we fear we won't be forgiven because we know we struggle with forgiving ourselves and others of their sins. Yet a child doesn't get caught up in all this. They have not been jaded by life and still accept that if they mess up their parents will still love them and so will God. They come unabashedly before God and sit on His knee and say, "I'm sorry for hurting my sister, please forgive me and help me do better." As adults we think we have to crawl on our bellies and grovel before the big God of the universe and then maybe He'll forgive us. But is that true? Or is that one of those lies the enemy has led us to believe? There is nothing we can do to earn forgiveness. The price was paid at Calvary. We don't have to offer a sacrifice to atone for our sins; we simply need to become as a child and come to our Heavenly Father who loves us enough to die for us and say, "I'm sorry for my sin, please help me to change so that I won't do it again." Then, in child-like faith, we need to accept, that just as we forgive our children when they do wrong, God forgives us!

If you have not become as a child and repented, I urge you to take a moment and do this right now. There is nothing as precious as going to your Heavenly Father and saying, "I'm sorry," and feeling His perfect, unending, all-powerful, unconditional, healing, forgiving love, sweeping over your soul. Casting your sins into the sea of forgetfulness, as far as the east is from the west (Psalm 103:12) you are forgiven. And just as your child comes to you each time they make a mistake and say, "I'm sorry," and you forgive them, remember, you, too, can approach the throne of grace and receive the same love and forgiveness. If your child has already begun to think nothing is pure, as in Titus 1:15, lead them in repentance. Model for them a pure life so they don't see hypocrisy in their home, and they will be more willing to accept any lifestyle changes you are implementing. Children are hungry for authenticity. Remember you, too, are still a child and your Father is looking down in love.

Except you become as a child…

Tips to help:

- Pray as a family and ask God to show you the things in *your* life that are not pure. He will reveal the areas that would hinder you from becoming as a child. Then ask Him to show you anything in your child's life that they are holding onto that would defile them. You may be surprised at what He will show you. It may seem hard at first for you and your child to give these things up, but remember that it is the pure

in heart that will see God. What a reward for obedience to purity!
- Open your home to your child's friends so you can get to know them.
- Stay current on the various media influencing your child and give appropriate guidance. Plugged In magazine is a great resource for this.
- Teach your child the power of repentance and forgiveness by modeling it for them.

Prayer: Oh, thank you Jesus for your power to cleanse us and make us new. As long as we are on this earth and in this flesh we will never truly be pure. However, we should strive to give you glory in all that we do and say. Father, help me to become as a child, so I will be an example to your child of a pure life devoted unto you. In your perfect name, Jesus, I pray, Amen.

Chapter 4

Lay Aside Every Weight
Hebrews 12:1

...let us lay aside every weight, and the sin which doth so easily beset us, and let us run with patience the race that is set before us,

There is a dangerous and common misconception we need to be aware of as parents, "Don't fight your kids on the small stuff." There are cases when this is true, such as, wearing a purple shirt with red pants. This may not be aesthetically pleasing, but it won't harm them. However, other "small stuff" has the ability to grow into a giant problem. In Hebrews, Paul exhorts us to "lay aside every weight." What is a "weight?" They are the "small" things that can "easily beset us" if we allow them into our lives. Violent video games, immodest clothing, sexually explicit movies, degrading music, cussing etc. may seem like "small" stuff compared to murder and sexual immorality, but if you don't handle the small things, they may become weights that can easily beset us. These are the things that are not expressly forbidden in scripture but are still easy to identify. The way you find out if it could be a weight is to ask, "Does that game, outfit, movie, joke etc. give glory to God?" This is a simple tool to use to decide if it is wise to allow your child to do something or not. Remember, "Whatsoever you do, do all to the glory of God."

How can the way we dress or how our child dresses matter? Does it cause people to look on you and lust? Or, does it allow people to see a countenance radiating the love of Christ? Why do video games matter? Do they edify the Spirit of God or a murderous, violent, hateful spirit? As I stated earlier, satan is subtle with how he kills our children today. If he can desensitize our children, he has them in his clutches. When violence, sex, and disrespectful attitudes are a common part of their life, they are no longer bothered by it, and the Truth no longer touches them. They no longer feel bad when they sin because their eyes and ears and hearts are being filled with it. Remember the story from chapter one of the TV show that was affecting my daughter? If I had not taken action and corrected the issue, her behavior would have become a part of her. Then the next level of disrespect and disobedience would have been that much easier to accept.

Today's mentality says, "It's just a book, how can it hurt me?" or "It's only a movie." How about, "This book/movie/song is about real life so how can it be wrong?" These are questions our kids ask. What we must be able to explain is what is behind these seemingly *small* things. There are those whose world-view is anti-Christ and they are not ashamed to market their dangerous beliefs to our children. In fact, some specifically target children in order to spread their message to a larger audience. They know if children read, listen, or watch it, most likely the parents will too. If not careful, unsuspecting parents may be allowing their children to be indoctrinated with a distorted view of our Savior.

Why are we allowing our children, while young and impressionable, to receive through various mediums the enemies lies? As intentional parents we must use discernment in what we allow our children to reach out and take hold of. Again, while we cannot hide our children from bad influences, we can make a point to teach them how to live in this world yet not be of it:

> Love not the world, neither the things that are in the world. If any man love the world, the love of the Father is not in him. For all that is in the world, the lust of the flesh, and the lust of the eyes, and the pride of life, is not of the Father, but is of the world. 1 John 2:15-16

Parents, to be able to ask your child if what he wants to do gives glory to God, you will have to examine your own life. You and your child will have to decide what is more important: living a life pleasing to God (Colossians 1:10) or enjoying the pleasures of sin for a season (Hebrews 11:25). As stated in the previous chapter, there is no age limit for being careful of what we see, hear, say, or do. If it applies to your child, it applies to you. The weights Paul tells us to get rid of are not sins per se; however, they are weights, and think of what the function of weights is. They weigh things down. The ways of God should set us free. His yoke is easy and His burden is light (Matthew 11:30).

You see, we are in this world but not of this world; we can't be weighed down and run a race!

> Do you not know that those who run in a race all run, but one receives the prize? Run in such a way that you may obtain it. And everyone who competes for the prize is temperate in all things. Now they do it to obtain a perishable crown, but we for an imperishable crown. 1 Corinthians 9:24-25 (NKJV)

Paul tells us if we're going to run THE race, then run it to win! I know people who are extremely disciplined in their pursuit to compete in marathons and decathlons. Day in and day out, no matter the weather conditions, they strive toward their goal to be conditioned and ready to compete. They have to train in all circumstances because the race may require that they compete in the same conditions. And they do all this for a "perishable crown!" How much more should we train, by rising early, no matter the circumstances to spend time with our Lord? The race we are in is one with an eternal prize, an "imperishable crown."

> Blessed is the man that endureth temptation: for when he is tried, he shall receive the crown of life, which the Lord hath promised to them that love him. James 1:12

> I press on to reach the end of the race and receive the heavenly prize for which God, through Christ Jesus, is calling us. Philippians 3:14 (NLT)

We have to "press" on! No matter how hard the trials seem, no matter how many fiery darts the enemy throws at us, we must press on toward the prize. Jesus never said it would be easy to serve him, in fact He tells us in John 15:20, "...The servant is not greater than his lord. If they have persecuted me, they will also persecute you;" We may not be persecuted in the same way as our Lord, but we can be assured trials will come our way:

> Beloved, think it not strange concerning the fiery trial which is to try you, as though some strange thing happened unto you: 1 Peter 4:12

> For thou, O God, hast proved us: thou hast tried us, as silver is tried. Psalm 66:10

How is silver tried? The Refiner uses a Refiner's fire so hot it causes the dross to separate from the liquid metal causing the impurities to raise to the surface so the Refiner can then remove the dross. (In the previous chapter we learned how important purity is to the Master.) As the dross is removed, the silver becomes purer, reflecting the image of the Refiner. "Take away the dross from the silver, and there shall come forth a vessel for the finer" (Proverbs 25:4). As one dictionary defines, dross is "something worthless!" Our Lord is The Silversmith of our life. In order to be silver that he can use to reflect His image, we have to get rid of the "weights," the "worthless" things in our life! To run The Race and obtain the prize we have to let Him remove the dross from our lives.

Another benefit to being *tried* is we learn patience: "Knowing this, that the trying of your faith worketh patience" (James 1:3). We are told to run the race with patience, not worrying about others or things that might be ahead of us in the race. We also should not look behind at where we have come from, but run with patience toward the prize. Patience is what you learn when you're tried and the dross is removed. After you have been tried, you understand it was for your good, and you learn to trust that the Silversmith knows what He is doing. Patience teaches you that the race is not necessarily to the swiftest but to the one who endures to the end. Runners training for a marathon learn to pace themselves, rather than sprint right out of the block only to wear out long before the finish line. As runners train for their race, they learn to focus on the goal no matter the conditions they are in. As Christians, patience helps you keep your eyes off the things around you which can so easily

Intentional Parenting

beset you; instead, you press on, ever striving for that imperishable crown.

As a parent, are you laying aside every weight and the sin that so easily besets you? Are you training up your child to lay aside these things? We are the parent, and it is up to us to set the example and teach them a more excellent Way. It is up to us to prune anything from our child's life that would hinder them as they train to run *The Race*.

Tips to help:

- Teach your child to ask, "If I do this would it give glory to God?" This is the easiest test to teach them to help them make good choices on their own.
- Take the time to listen to the music they like, watch the shows they watch, and even get to know who they hang out with to determine if they could be weights.
- If your children are still young enough to depend upon you for purchasing power, then make sure you are using that "power" to support what encourages purity, not what the world is trying to tell your child is good.
- Talk to your child. Explain to them the reason for the changes and show them through your own life that you, too, only want to do what is pleasing unto the Lord.

Prayer: Precious Savior, you told us your yoke is easy and your burden is light. You don't want us to be weighed down with the cares of this life. Help me to lay aside every weight that would hold me or my child down. We want to be able to run this race to the finish and receive our crown someday. We want to hear you say, "Well done my good and faithful servant." Lord, I need your help to give up the things that are not pleasing to you. Thank you for the trials that remove the worthless things in my life so I can be patient and endure to the finish line. Help me to be what my child needs me to be, and I know you'll take care of the rest. I ask this in Jesus name, Amen.

Chapter 5

I Formed Thee
Jeremiah 1:5

Before I formed thee in the belly I knew thee; and before thou camest forth out of the womb I sanctified thee, and I ordained thee a prophet unto the nations.

Think on that passage for a moment. We know that the Word is given to instruct us, to teach us of God and His ways. Through this scripture we know, like Jeremiah, that before we were formed He knew us and created us for a purpose. Just as God created everything else in the world, He created you! Just as He created you with a purpose in mind, He created your child. Parents, we must teach our children that God knew them even before they were formed. They need to know He formed them, that He "made all the delicate, inner parts of my body and knit me together in my mother's womb," (Psalm 139:13 NLT) and gave them life because He has great plans for them.

I am very aware that my children are not truly mine. Yes, God has entrusted me and their daddy to train them up but they are truly His children. We were just the vehicle He used to bring them into this world. He knew our girls before He formed them in my womb and He has a plan for their life. He loves them more and knows them even better than we do: "But now, O LORD, thou art our father; we are the clay, and thou our potter; and we all are the work of thy hand" (Isaiah 64:8).

We are all clay on the potter's wheel, being formed and transformed into His image (2 Corinthians 3:18). The beauty of a vessel being molded by the Potter's hand is made evident in a child. They are just beginning to take shape of what they will become. You see, God knew us all before we were born. To Him we are clay, and a new vessel can be used just as easily as an old one. It is the willingness that makes the difference. God used an eight year old king to fight the evil of his day (2 Kings 22), a young man named David to kill a giant (1 Samuel 17), a young servant girl to reveal God's healing power to the enemy (2 Kings 5:2-4), and He used a young boy's lunch to feed the 5,000 (John 6:9). How were these young girls and boys able to do these things? Because they had been intentionally parented! Their parents understood God's command to teach them His laws and statutes. Their parents had equipped them to discern right from wrong, good from evil and not be ashamed to speak up when needed. Wouldn't you like to be the parent who prepares your child for the day (packs their lunch), and because they are prepared they are chosen to be part of a great miracle!?

We must be careful not to underestimate what our children are capable of doing when in the Potter's hands. Who would ever expect a child to lay hands on someone while praying for them to be healed (Mark 16:18) and it be done? Who expects children to usher in God's Spirit through their praise and worship? Who thinks that a child is capable of slaying a giant? God does! We know that God does not look on the outward but on the heart (1 Samuel 16:7). When I see children serving the Lord I think of 1 Corinthians 1:27, "But God hath chosen the foolish things of the world to confound the wise; and God hath chosen the weak things of the world to confound the things which are mighty." I also love the prophecy in Psalm 8:2, "Out of the mouth of babes and sucklings hast thou ordained strength because of thine enemies, that thou mightest still the enemy and the avenger." Then in Matthew 21: 15-16 we are told of its fulfillment:

> And when the chief priests and scribes saw the wonderful things that he did, and the children crying in the temple, and saying, Hosanna to the son of David; they were sore displeased, And said unto him, Hearest thou what these say? And Jesus saith unto them, Yea; have ye never read, Out of the mouth of babes and sucklings thou hast perfected praise?

Intentional Parenting

Notice when the unbelievers saw what Jesus did, and heard the children praising Him, they didn't like it! He responded to their displeasure by reminding them of the prophecy when He said, "...out of the mouths of children praise is perfected!"

Parent, you have been given the greatest gift you could ever have; "Children are a gift from the LORD; they are a reward from him" (Psalm 127:3 NLT). The Potter fashioned your child and chose to reward you with this *gift*. What are you doing with your *gift*? Are you being an intentional parent? Are you taking the time to tie them to Jesus so He can mold them into the vessel He desires them to be? Are you parenting with the intent that your child will serve the Lord with all their heart, soul, mind, and strength? When you parent this way, you are equipping your child to be a David, Josiah, or an Esther of their day.

The analogy in scripture of God as the Potter and us as the clay is so wonderful because it gives me a visual of the "hands-on" God who created me. In fact, this description of us as vessels is so powerful I once used it in a teacher training for our church's children's ministry. I gave each teacher a container of play-dough as well as a small clay pot. I asked each of them to use their play-dough to fashion their own little pot. It was fun to witness the vessels each teacher created. Some did their very best to create one that looked just like their sample. Others added embellishments that made them much prettier. The one consistent thing I witnessed from each *potter* was that they all had to make adjustments to their creations.

Intentional Parenting

Once they were all done fashioning their pots, I asked them to take a look at the store-bought, hardened, clay pots. I had purposely purchased several pots that had either cracks or even chunks missing from them. I asked those with broken pots to fix them. They proceeded to take their play-dough and fill in the cracks and holes as best they could. I then asked them to tell me whether it was easier to fix a mistake in the play-dough pots or the ones that were already hardened. Of course, they said the play-dough.

Besides the fact that each one had fun playing with the play-dough, they learned the important lesson of God being the Potter and we the clay. Our children are like the play-dough, they are soft and pliable, able to be molded into whatever the Potter wants them to be. As adults, we are more like the clay pot that was already hardened. Yes, it could still be fixed, the cracks could be filled and hidden, but they were still there. The play-dough pots were able to be corrected and the mistakes smoothed out into the results the creator desired. It is always easier to work with clay when it is soft and pliable; therefore, we must be intentional parents and begin to mold the vessels God has given us while they are young. A new vessel is soft, pliable, and able to yield to pressure. This is why the influences upon their young lives, both good and bad, can have such a profound effect. If they are yielding to good pressures in their life, they will be strengthened; however, if the pressures are for bad, this will cause deformities in their structure. We have been called as parents to apply the appropriate *pressure* to help strengthen God's vessel.

When God gives you the gift of a child, He has already formed the vessel into the design He wants it to become. It's up to you to see that as the vessel hardens it does not gather impurities that can cause it to crack under the pressure of firing. Think of impurities as being those "weights" we learned about earlier. Once clay has been shaped into the desired form, it is not safe from dents or scratches until it has been fired. If it happens to get a dent or even fall and get out of its original shape, it can still go through a process of reshaping. Its integrity is still intact. Once a vessel is fired, if it should fall, it can break and though glued back together and perhaps painted over, that break is still there. Thankfully, our Heavenly Father, The Potter, is faithful to not only put a broken vessel back together but make it like new! The process though is very painful for the vessel as well as The Potter. How much easier it is for The Potter, when He is allowed to work through us parents, to make corrections and small repairs while our children are pliable. Jeremiah describes this beautifully:

> Then I went down to the potter's house, and there he was, making something at the wheel. And the vessel that he made of clay was marred in the hand of the potter; so he made it again into another vessel, as it seemed good to the potter to make. Jeremiah 18:3-4 (NKJV)

Parent, the Potter has great plans for the vessel he has entrusted to you. Each vessel the Potter creates has been given unique characteristics designed to give glory to its Creator. As you get to know your child you will begin to see these characteristics. They are the gifts and talents your child has been given for His glory and purpose.

My oldest daughter happens to have a talent for being quite strong-willed. I say that with humor, but am quite serious about it being a talent. I admit she has had difficulties in the obedience department and with tears she has asked me why it's hard for her to "just obey." I have taught her that the same will that causes her problems, is also a great strength because it will help her stand strong when temptations come. Yes, it can also be a weakness if she is not clinging to Jesus. This strong-will can also lead her astray by making it difficult to submit to authority. This is when it takes determination from her daddy and me to make sure she sees the error in her behavior. Thankfully, because she is being trained to serve the Lord, we can take her to His Word and allow her to see the truth regarding her behavior. Her strong-will has already come in handy when she has had to stand up for herself and her convictions. I don't know how the Potter will use my daughter's talents, but I do know I can be intentional in how I help her develop her gifts. When the time comes for Him to use His vessel, she will be ready.

My youngest daughter has been given the gifts of joy and encouragement. She lights up any room she's in! We have been told how her joyfulness and kind words have made a difference in the lives she touches. Her daddy and I are being very intentional to teach her to use the power of words to build others up and not tear them down. I believe for every gift the Potter gives, the enemy tempts us to use it for bad. Just as my oldest daughter has to be careful that her strong-will does not cause disobedience, my youngest has to be careful of her tongue! That same tongue that was created to encourage can pierce when she is not careful. We need to be diligent in teaching these things to our children, so they will be aware of what they are doing and careful to use their gifts for good. What an incredible honor, to be entrusted with a unique, one of a kind, priceless gift, our children!

As you strive to train your child intentionally, part of that training has to be encouraging and guiding them in discovering their gifts. Then you can help your child develop them. Do they love to sing, dance, read, write, play ball? Are they sensitive to others feelings or hurts? These are just a few of the many ways our children can exhibit the gifts within themselves. All of these things can be used for God's glory. Yes, even playing ball! They can give God thanks for the talent to make good plays, and if given a position of respect, they can use it to share God's love with others. Even if they have a bad game their attitude about it can give glory to the One who is always cheering them on. If they understand they were formed by God, and He has a plan for their life, they have a better chance of respecting themselves and of being careful what they do with the gifts they've been given. Then they will be added to the list of those who did mighty things for the Lord while young.

Prayer: Lord you are the Potter, the one who formed me and my child. I know you have created us for the purpose of giving you glory and to use the gifts that are within us for your Kingdom. Help me to know the gifts you have given my child and show me ways to encourage them to use those gifts now while they are young. I know that age is not a factor with you, and I don't want to be guilty of limiting your creation. Thank you Father for helping me see my child as you see them. In Jesus name I pray, Amen.

Chapter 6

The Word Equips
2 Timothy 3:15-17 (NLT)

You have been taught the Holy Scriptures from childhood, and they have given you the wisdom to receive the salvation that comes by trusting in Christ Jesus. All Scripture is inspired by God and is useful to teach us what is true and to make us realize what is wrong in our lives. It corrects us when we are wrong and teaches us to do what is right. God uses it to prepare and equip his people to do every good work.

Over the years my husband and I have faced challenging times with our girls. We do our best to teach them what God has to say about the issues they are struggling with. It is important to begin imparting the Word into our children's lives "from childhood" so they can receive the "salvation that comes by trusting in Jesus."

During a period when my daughter was dealing with a sprit of fear at bedtime, I taught her scriptures to overcome it. It's natural for children to have some fears at night; it's dark, they're alone and hear strange noises. It's easy for their imaginations to go a bit crazy. One scripture I taught her to think on is Philippians 4:8, "Finally, brethren, whatsoever things are true...think on these things."

Rather than dwelling on what she was imagining, lies, I stressed to her to think on what is true. She knew she was safe in her home in her bed, and that in reality there was nothing bad going on. Being armed with the Word and being comforted by her Bible lying open on the table next to her bed helped her to overcome and rest safely in God's arms. She is learning she can trust in Jesus for all her needs. By learning to trust in Him for protection and comfort she is also learning how very much He loves her.

Another example of the power in knowing the Word was displayed one day when my daughter was dealing with condemnation. A few days before this event took place, I had asked the Lord to help me understand the difference between conviction and condemnation. As I listened to her frustration with herself, for bad behavior she had earlier that day, I understood she was condemning herself because I had a tendency to do the same thing when I made a mistake. I immediately spoke to her that she should not do that. It is the enemy wanting her to feel bad about herself. I said, "God wants you to feel sorry [or convicted] about what you did wrong, not bad about yourself!" Well, as I was helping my daughter, God helped His daughter, me, understand the difference between conviction and condemnation. He brought to mind a scripture I had read only days before, Psalm 103:14, "For he knoweth our frame; he remembereth that we are dust." God does not expect us to be perfect, so we shouldn't expect it of ourselves. Wow!! You see, if I was not arming myself daily with God's Word, He could not have brought to mind that scripture to allow me to minister to my daughter.

My youngest daughter's favorite scripture is, "I can do all things through Christ which strengtheneth me" (Philippians 4:13). She finds comfort in knowing the Lord is there to help her. When she says "I can't do it," I remind her she can with Christ's help. Children must know in their hearts they can call His name, and He will be there to give them courage. They can conquer through Him:

> Yet in all these things we are more than conquerors through Him who loved us. For I am persuaded that neither death nor life, nor angels nor principalities nor powers, nor things present nor things to come, nor height nor depth, nor any other created thing, shall be able to separate us from the love of God which is in Christ Jesus our Lord. Romans 8:37-39

No matter what they face, nothing can separate them from the love of God. He will always be there to strengthen them when they call on His name.

The day will come when our children will have to take a stand for what is pure and gives God glory. They will not be able to do this without their feet firmly planted upon the Word of God. Knowing truths such as: Jesus died for us that we might live (1 Peter 2:24, 1 John 4:9) and knowing He suffered in all ways in order to help us (Hebrews 2:17-18), will help them as they face the difficulties of life. We know by Jesus' own example the Word is powerful, so we need to be intentional in teaching our child to hide His Word in their hearts (Psalm 119:11). It's not good enough for us parents to know the Word, but not our children. Our sword cannot always defeat their enemies; they must be armed with their own swords. It is always easier to defend yourself if you have some kind of weapon, but for that weapon to be effective you have to be trained in how to use it. Those who have mastered martial arts and have learned to use their body as a weapon had to be taught how! We cannot expect our children to be able to make wise choices if they have not been taught God's Word! We cannot expect them to live a life unto God if they have not learned what His commands are. We can only expect them to be strong enough to stand up to the enemy if they have been equipped and trained with the only weapon that can defeat him; the Word!

The Word must be hid in their hearts while children so when the enemy comes they will be armed and ready to discern what is truth and what are lies.

How can our children stand a chance against hell's deceptions if we do not arm them with the Truth? What is the Truth? God's Word is Truth! Jesus is the way the truth and the life (John 14:6). Just as we feed our bodies each day we must feed our spirits "daily bread," the Word of God. This is why we must be diligent and feed our children the Bread of Life from sun-up to sun-down for there is no other way for them to be armed for warfare.

Warfare? Yes, warfare. In America our children may not be carrying machine guns, or fighting off an attack from an invading country, but they are in a battle nonetheless. The warfare our children face in our culture comes in more subtle ways. Parents, you are responsible for protecting your child from these attacks by what is unseen; "For we wrestle not against flesh and blood, but against principalities, against powers, against the rulers of the darkness of this world, against spiritual wickedness in high places" (Ephesians 6:12). The enemy has packaged a sinful life in such a pretty way that children cannot help but want it! It is your job to peel off that pretty covering and expose sin for what it is: a path that leads to destruction. Satan has used many means over the centuries to kill our children: Throughout history pagan religions have taught sacrificing children to false gods. While the children of Israel were in Egypt Pharaoh ordered all the boys born to the Hebrews to be thrown into the Nile (Exodus 1:22), and in Jesus day King Herod also ordered the baby boys in Bethlehem to be murdered (Matthew 2:16). Today is no different it is just more subtle. Today it is not only physical death, such as abortion, but spiritual death that takes place, and as God's Word teaches, a life of sin is death (Romans 6:23).

Jesus, being our perfect example, taught us how to fight the enemy. When He was tempted by satan, He countered each time with a scripture (Matthew 4:1-10, Luke 4:2-12). Ephesians 6:17b plainly states, "take... the sword of the Spirit, which is the word of God:"

> For the word of God is quick, and powerful, and sharper than any twoedged sword, piercing even to the dividing asunder of soul and spirit, and of the joints and marrow, and is a discerner of the thoughts and intents of the heart. Hebrews 4:12

> I have written unto you, young men, because ye are strong, and the word of God abideth in you, and ye have overcome the wicked one. 1 John 2:14b

Not only will the Word defeat the enemies without, it will reveal the enemy within…our thoughts and desires. As we learn God's Word and hide it in our hearts, it will reveal to us those things within us that need to be cut out. It convicts us regarding what is wrong in our life. Our children will begin to make choices based upon the Word that is hid in their hearts. How much easier it will be for our children to say no to sin and overcome the wicked one, when they have His Word in their heart and their sword in their hand.

Intentional Parenting

Tips to help:

- Teach by example, the most powerful form of teaching our children. If they see you reading your Bible, they will be more apt to read theirs.
- Make it fun! When children are young they can learn the Word through the many wonderful songs created to teach children scriptures. Or, play games as a family like Bible Outburst.
- Repetition. The more your children read or hear scriptures the better they'll learn them.
- As soon as they can read, give them their own age appropriate Bible to read. Bibles with lots of pictures are great! As they grow older present them with a devotional Bible to encourage daily reading. The New Living Translation is great for children and teens.
- Work as a family to memorize a new scripture each week—hang it on the fridge where everyone will see it and hold each other accountable to learn it.
- Pray the Word. When you pray with your child, season it with scripture.

Prayer: Thank you Jesus for your Word! Thank you for teaching us how to defeat the enemy that is within and without. You have armed us with your Word, the sword of the spirit. Please help us to hide your Word in our hearts and to teach our children the importance of hiding it in theirs. In your powerful name, Jesus I pray, Amen.

Chapter 7

A Child of God From the Womb
Judges 13:3-5

And the angel of the LORD appeared unto the woman, and said unto her, Behold now, thou art barren, and bearest not: but thou shalt conceive, and bear a son. Now therefore beware, I pray thee, and drink not wine nor strong drink, and eat not any unclean thing: For, lo, thou shalt conceive, and bear a son; and no razor shall come on his head: for the child shall be a Nazarite unto God from the womb: and he shall begin to deliver Israel out of the hand of the Philistines.

Moms, this passage offers tremendous insight into how important we are to the spiritual calling of our children. Before Samson was even conceived he had a mother who was first called to separate herself so that her child would be dedicated unto the Lord "from the womb." This reinforces what we learned from Jeremiah (1:5): God knows us even before we are formed and He creates us with a purpose! Through the story of Samson, as well as many others, we discover the significance of a mother's walk with her Lord.

What a woman Samson's mother must have been to be trusted by the Lord to obey his command for her life and her child. We know from the book of Judges that during this period of Israel, the Israelites were doing "evil in the Lord's sight." I'm sure this contributed to the surprise of being visited by an angel of the Lord and the fear that they were going to die (Judges 12:22). Yet Samson's mother understood who the visitor was and recognized the honor that had been bestowed her and obeyed the Lord. Because of her obedience to the Word of the Lord, her son became a judge of Israel and delivered Israel from the hand of the Philistines. Was Samson perfect? No; but he did fulfill the purpose God created him for. And it all began with a mother fulfilling what *she* was created for.

Another beautiful example of a mother who had a profound effect on her son is Hannah. Hannah, too, had trouble conceiving, yet her faith in her Lord never waned. In 1 Samuel chapter 1, we learn her story, as well as the beginning of the story of Samuel. In verse 11, we see her cry out to the Lord in anguish and make a vow to the Lord: If He should give her a son, she will return him to the Lord, and as a sign that he is dedicated to the Lord, his hair will not be cut.

Further on in verse 15, after being accused by Eli, the priest, that she is drunk, she replies, "I have not been drinking wine or anything stronger!" Does that sound familiar? Like Samson's mother, Hannah separated herself so that her son would be dedicated unto God even from the womb. We know that each year Hannah went faithfully with her husband to offer the yearly sacrifice, and it was there that she cried out to her God. Even when the world around her "did what was right in his own eyes" (Judges 17:6) she remained faithful to the Lord. When years had passed without conceiving she remained steadfast in her faith to the Lord. The Lord must have looked upon Hannah and recognized a woman with unwavering faith and a desire for her child to serve the Lord. God knew, for His child Samuel to become all He created him to be, he would need a mother strong enough to train him up in the way he should go. We can imagine during that precious time Hannah spent with Samuel, she poured out her love for her Lord and His faithfulness to answer her cry. We can imagine her holding him and preparing herself as well as the child for the day she would fulfill her promise to return him to the Lord. Shouldn't we all practice this? Isn't this what every parent should desire, for their child to grow up in God's service? This doesn't mean they have to become pastors; it means living for the Lord and obeying His Word. Thankfully, God does not require us to leave our children at the Temple only to visit a few times a year, but we should parent them as if we were.

These mothers understood the importance of their role in their child's life, and we know that both of these boys went on to be used mightily by the Lord. Samson and Samuel had been intentionally parented with the goal being that they would serve the Lord. These mothers did not simply look at giving birth as something they were supposed to do; they understood they had an important role in preparing a child to serve the Lord. This is why the "child Samuel" was able to "minister before the Lord" (1Samuel 2:18).

Imagine being a Hebrew woman during the time in Egypt when all the boys born were to be killed. This is the time in which Moses' mother, Jochebed, gave birth to him. Rather than suffer this, she bravely gave her child to the Lord (Exodus 2). She must have understood that her son was not just her and her husband's child, but being God's child she would trust the Lord to take care of him. As a mommy myself, I think of the strength of her faith in a loving God and how her heart must have ached as she gave her child to Him. No matter our love for God and our faith in Him, it is not easy to give up our child. But, because of her faith and determination to save her baby, God was not only able to save him, he also gave him back to his mother to nurse and train up to know the Lord. Because of the years Moses spent with Jochebed, when the day came for the Lord to reveal Himself as the God of Abraham, Isaac, and Jacob, Moses understood whose presence he was standing in (Exodus 3:5-6).

As a mother, the hardest thing you will have to do is give your child back to God. It sounds easy.

After all if you can survive childbirth what's the big deal about saying, "Here Lord, take my child?" But once you have held that child and loved that child and spent sleepless nights with that child, that child is yours! It's harder to think of them as being God's. But then those times come that you don't understand and don't quite know what to do. This is how it begins: First, you do everything you know to do. If the problem remains, you ask your mother and sisters and friends if they have any ideas. You try them, but that doesn't work either. Next, you go out and buy a new book on child development and find the chapter on your problem and realize that isn't working either! Finally, in desperation, you go to the One who has been waiting and watching you do all this, the One who created your child, and you cry out, "Lord, help! What do I do? I've tried everything and nothing works!" And the Lord says, "Trust in me and lean not on your own understanding" (Proverbs 3:5). Because you are so worn out from all your other attempts you say, "Okay."

Then within a short while, something changes... you don't even know when, or why, but suddenly your child is no longer struggling with that thing that seemed like a mountain. Wow, God really does know what He's doing if we would just let Him! We have to remember our child is ultimately God's, and because they were created by a loving Creator, He can fix His creation. Everything we buy comes with information on who created it; if there is a problem we go to that company. We don't send our TV off to be repaired by a plumber or our computer to an auto shop; we send it to the one who built it because they know what it needs to work properly. If we learn to do this with our children, our job as mothers will be much easier. Notice I didn't say easy, just easier. It is difficult to fully trust the Lord with our children because we hate seeing them hurt, but sometimes this is what they need in order to learn their lesson.

Tough love is tough on everyone involved, even God because He loves us so much. But when you have given your child to God and have taken everything to Him in prayer, you can rest in the promise that He will never leave us nor forsake us. I have seen mothers try their best to *save* their children, and it didn't work. It was only when they got completely out of the way and let God decide what was best that the child finally understood what path they were on and returned to the Way they had been taught. Thankfully, they had been taught the Way so when the Lord did His work, they understood it was the hand of the Lord reaching out to save them.

We also find a powerful model of a mother's influence in Lois and Eunice:

> I remember your genuine faith, for you share the faith that first filled your grandmother Lois and your mother, Eunice. And I know that same faith continues strong in you. 2 Timothy 1:5 (NLT)

> But you must remain faithful to the things you have been taught. You know they are true, for you know you can trust those who

taught you. You have been taught the holy Scriptures from childhood, and they have given you the wisdom to receive the salvation that comes by trusting in Christ Jesus. 2 Timothy 3:14-15 (NLT)

What an incredible heritage Timothy was born into and proof that mothers have profound influence upon their children's spiritual training. What a blessing it must have been to these women to see Timothy grow into a man of strong faith! Because they understood the importance of their child knowing the Word of God, they gave him wisdom to receive salvation! What peace and joy to know your child is saved!

I cannot address the importance of motherhood without also looking at Ruth and her mother-in-law Naomi. The first chapter of Ruth tells us there was a famine in the land of Judah, and because of this, Naomi, her husband, and two sons went to the country of Moab to live. While living in Moab, Naomi's husband died leaving just her and her two sons. Her sons went on to marry women from the country of Moab, where they were still dwelling, and after about ten years, her sons died as well. After losing her husband and sons, Naomi hears the famine has ended, and decides she wants to go home to the land of Judah. In love, she told both of her daughters-in-law they could return to their families. At first they both said they would go with her, but after releasing them again to go home, it was only her daughter-in-law Ruth who refused to leave her. Naomi did not make it easy for Ruth to remain with her until Ruth told her this:

> Don't ask me to leave you and turn back. Wherever you go, I will go; wherever you live, I will live. Your people will be my people, and your God will be my God. Wherever you die, I will die, and there I will be buried. May the LORD punish me severely if I allow anything but death to separate us!" When Naomi saw that Ruth was determined to go with her, she said nothing more. Ruth 1:16-18 (NLT)

Ruth was not Naomi's blood daughter. Yet she had obviously made a significant impression on Ruth during their years together, and Ruth didn't want to lose what she had found. Ruth had found the Lord! Naomi's life must have reflected the Lord in such a distinct way that Ruth didn't want to return to the gods she had known before; she wanted Naomi's God! This is the effect an adoptive mom, step mom, or mother-in-law can have on her children and their spouses. You can reflect God's love in such a way that even if grown, these children will make your God their God. And just as Samson and Samuel went on to do great things for the Lord, this daughter by marriage goes on to become the great-grandmother of King David! Surely, Ruth had a hand in passing down to her son, who passed it to his son, and so on, that the God of her mother-in-law Naomi is the one true God, and He should be loved with all your heart, soul, mind, and strength! Ruth is even honored by being one of the few women mentioned in the book of Matthew in the genealogy of Jesus, and all because there was a godly mother in her life.

Mothers, we have been assigned a very important role. We must be intentional in training our children in the Way they should go. Every child has been created for a purpose. Your role as mommy to that child is part of God's plan for both of you. He gave you your child because there is something about you that God needs to use as part of your child's training. There is something only you can give them. No matter the age of your child, you can have a profound impact on your child's life. Don't let the regret of past mistakes hold you back from being the mommy you want to be. We all make mistakes. Instead, do your best every day to be a godly woman and teach your child a new Way. God is always there willing to help make up the difference for our short-comings. Your example will teach your daughters how to be a godly wife and mommy, and you will be teaching your sons what to expect in a wife. What an honor to be trusted by God with his creations!

It saddens me that in today's culture, you find the attitude that unless women work outside the home, they must not be fulfilled. This is such a lie of the enemy. Now, I'm very aware that there are millions of working moms who do not have a choice and would stay at home with their children if they could. I respect the load they carry. I also know many wonderful mothers that work all day and come home to a houseful of children and do their best to train them up in the way they should go. I want to speak to the stay-at-home moms that have bought into the lie that to stay at home and be a full time mommy means you are less than those who work outside the home. If you have chosen this path, you should be proud of your accomplishments as a wife and mommy, and never be ashamed to say, "I'm a stay at home mom." You are fulfilling Titus 2:4-5 (NLT):

> These older women must train the younger women to love their husbands and their children, to live wisely and be pure, to work in their homes, to do good, and to be submissive to their husbands. Then they will not bring shame on the Word of God.

Being submissive does not mean you are a doormat to be walked on. It means you understand you are not the head and that by letting the man fulfill his role, he is the one that has to answer to God for any wrong doing. It is liberating for me to know I can give my husband my opinion, and then whatever he decides, it is on his head! As my husband likes to say, "I'm the head, but she is the neck who turns it." God has given us our husbands as a covering, and we are submitting to our Lord when we submit to his authority (Ephesians 5:22-23).

Remember: If you have sons, you are modeling to them what to expect from their wife and if you have daughters, how to be a keeper of the home. Will your son look for a wife who is defiant and quarrelsome (Proverbs 27:15)? Or, will he choose a wife who respects and loves him? Will your daughters learn from your example to respect their husband? Or, are you teaching them to argue and complain (Proverbs 21:19)? Hopefully, because of your example, your son will choose a wife that is reflected in Proverbs 18:22, "The man who finds a wife finds a treasure, and he receives favor from the Lord." And hopefully, your daughter will be a "treasure" to her husband. What kind of legacy are you leaving behind?

It was through a woman that the Savior came, and that same Savior made her a mother. Through childbirth we fulfill a role that, according to 1 Timothy 2:15, "saves" us. Through this role redemption came for the sin committed in the Garden. Thank God for the miracle of motherhood!

Tips to help:

- Spend time enjoying your child, get to know them and make memories. This can be making cookies together (even boys like this!), gardening, bike riding, reading, snuggle up and watch a favorite movie, playing basketball. It's not about the activity; it's that you are together.
- Spend time with God. As a mom you need to have your daily time with your Lord so you can be prepared for what that day brings.
- Cultivate friendships with other mothers so you can learn from their experiences and share your own.

Prayer: Thank you Jesus for calling me to be a mother. Help me to be the mother Your child needs me to be. Help me to trust in You for how to parent and lean not on my own understanding. I want to be a mother who reflects your glory in all that I do. Your ways are perfect, and I know you love our child even more than I do. Thank you for your Word that will be my guide (Psalm 119:133). In the lovely name of Jesus I pray, Amen.

Chapter 8

Walk as Thy Father Walked
1 Kings 9:4-5

And if thou wilt walk before me, as David thy father walked, in integrity of heart, and in uprightness, to do according to all that I have commanded thee, and wilt keep my statutes and my judgments: Then I will establish the throne of thy kingdom upon Israel for ever, as I promised to David thy father, saying, There shall not fail thee a man upon the throne of Israel.

Father: Provider, Protector, Strength, Counselor, Leader, Encourager, Powerful, Wise, Loving, Caring, Compassionate, Comforter and Friend. These are all the roles of a father. These beautiful descriptions could also be describing our "everlasting Father" (Isaiah 9:6). This is why it is so important for fathers to be the spiritual leaders of their home; fathers are exemplifying the very character of God!

David was many things: shepherd, warrior, husband, king, but the most important was, father. He was not perfect in all his ways like our heavenly Father, but according to 1 Kings 9:4-5 he walked "in integrity of heart, and in uprightness." As Solomon's father, David was the one God referred to as the example of how Solomon should live and what to expect in return; the establishment of his throne forever. All Solomon had to do was walk as his father walked.

When Solomon was dedicating the Temple of the Lord he turned to the people and said, "And it was in the heart of David my father to build an house for the name of the LORD God of Israel" (1 Kings 8:17). Even though David was not able to build the Temple, he was able to instill in his son Solomon the desire and determination to fulfill his father's dream of honoring the Lord. David's love for the Lord spilled over to Solomon and Solomon completed what David began. What a tremendous legacy to pass on to a child. What splendid footsteps Solomon had to follow. What footsteps are you leaving behind?

In Ephesians 6:4 (NLT) fathers are told, "…do not provoke your children to anger by the way you treat them. Rather bring them up with the discipline and instruction that comes from the Lord." Fathers, this is a heavy responsibility. Thankfully, our heavenly Father has left us with examples and lessons of how to fulfill this role. Let's first look to at the example in Job 1:1 of a father who "was blameless—a man of complete integrity," Job:

> And it was so, when the days of their feasting were gone about, that Job sent and sanctified them, [his children] and rose up early in the morning, and offered burnt offerings according to the number of them all: for Job said, It may be that my sons have sinned, and cursed God in their hearts. Thus did Job continually. Job 1:5

Here is a father who continually made sure that his children were covered by God's grace and mercy. It was his role as the spiritual covering for his family to offer sacrifice to the Lord and ask for forgiveness. Today, we can go boldly to the throne of grace (Hebrews 4:16) without offering sacrifices on an altar to God. However, you should still be sacrificing daily for your children to be saved. This sacrifice could be: Making sure you spend time with your children. Instead of sleeping until the last possible moment before getting ready for work, rise up early and pray for your family. It can be a sacrifice of the fanciest car or the biggest house because you would rather have a job that allows you time with your family.

When you are gone, what will remain and be a testament of your life? Your children. These are the treasures you can lay up that neither moth nor rust will corrupt (Matthew 6:20). Your possessions will wear out or be sold off, but your children's lives will remain.

Intentional Parenting

Elkanah is another example of a godly husband and father. In the previous chapter we looked at Samuel's mother, and just as important as her influence was upon Samuel so was his father's. We are told in 1 Samuel 1:3, "And this man went up out of his city yearly to worship and to sacrifice unto the LORD of hosts in Shiloh." We know from this he was faithful to obey the laws of the Lord. Like Job, he was the priest of his home in leading his family to follow the Law. We also know, as the head of his family, that he led them in worship of the Lord: "And they rose up in the morning early, and worshipped before the LORD, and returned, and came to their house to Ramah" (1 Samuel 1:19a). He didn't stay home while his wife and children went off to church; rather, he led them to it!

His faith in the Lord and his love for his wife Hannah is evident in his support of Hannah. He understood when you make a vow to the Lord you must keep it. He strengthened and encouraged his wife to do a very hard thing. He did not try to dissuade her or keep her from honoring her promise to God. Instead, when the time came to take Samuel to the house of the Lord, he was right beside her. In chapter 2 we are told she would take a coat to her son each year when she and her husband went to offer the yearly sacrifice. This was not a woman who had to go to church alone and worship alone. This was a woman blessed to have a husband who loved her very much and was a godly influence in her life. This gave her strength to be the mother she had to be to Samuel. Fathers, you not only directly influence your children by your behavior toward them, but indirectly, by your behavior toward their mother.

The enemy has been quite successful in his assault on fathers. If you believe commercials and television shows, you would believe that men are only good at drinking beer, lusting after women, and being lazy. Our society has managed to shift from one led by fathers to one led by mothers and this is not the way it should be. Just as only a woman can give birth to a child, only a man can be a father and head of his home. No scripture teaches that women are the head, or lead the family, or should be the ruler of their home. This is a role intended for men. This is stated very plainly in 1 Corinthians 11:3: "But I would have you know, that the head of every man is Christ; and the head of the woman is the man."

This may not be very popular with some women, but men this is your place. However, this is not a position to abuse, as we find in Ephesians 5:25, you are to "love your wives, even as Christ also loved the church, and gave himself for it." This is a powerful love and a powerful model of what is expected of you. If, as husband and wife, our roles are in their proper order, then our house will be in order and our children will be blessed by it.

There is an account in scripture of a family known as the Rechabites. I enjoy this story because it illustrates the influence of a father's instruction. Rechab taught his son, who taught his son, and so on, that they should never drink wine or build houses or plant crops, but instead be as strangers in the land. The Lord knowing this, had Jeremiah go to where the Rechabites were living, invite them to the house of the Lord, and offer them wine. Now this may seem strange, but God was trying to prove a point to his people in Judah. When the Rechabites were offered the wine, they refused it and explained it was because their father Rechab had charged them, their wives, and children not to drink wine! We know God was very impressed by this faithfulness to honor their father because He blessed them by saying they would always have descendants that would serve Him. His people in Judah, on the other hand, who had not obeyed their own Heavenly Father's commands, were punished. You can read the full account of this in Jeremiah 35.

Fathers, even if your children are not yours by birth, your ability to have a profound influence upon them is the same. We know this is true from Esther 2:7b (NLT): "When her father and mother died, Mordecai adopted her into his family and raised her as his own daughter." Mordecai did not treat Esther as anything less than his own. Because of his love, and training her up in the way she should go, she went on to be used as an instrument in the Lord's hand to save His people. It says that even while queen she continued to honor Mordecai just as she had when living at home (Esther 2:19-20). The fact that Mordecai refused to bow to any man, other than his king or the Lord even though it could mean punishment, shows us what a great man of faith he was. It is obvious by Esther's behavior this faith was handed down to her from Mordecai, for she, too, was willing to do the right thing no matter the cost. We are told in chapter 4 verse 15, she called for the people to go on a fast for her. She understood the dangerous position she was in and also understood it was from God that wisdom and guidance would come. Because of a man who adopted a child and raised her as his own, a nation was saved.

While serving in our church I came to know two teenage girls who are sisters. I saw in them something rare today: modesty and respect for themselves and others. I spent some time with them asking how their father had influenced them. I would like to share what they had to say. First, they told me that the song "Daddy's Hands", by Holly Dunn, pretty much sums up their dad. They told me he makes them feel safe: always making sure to pray with them before leaving in the morning, praying for them to choose good friends, and for God to send good friends to them. He also prays for them every night at bedtime, speaking into their lives who they are in Christ. They told me he not only tells them he loves them but also shows them. He laughs at their jokes, even when they are corny, and supports them by attending their many band and sport events. Their parents have always made attending church a priority and have made a point to get to know the other parents of the kids they hang around so they know what kind of influence they could be on them. They told me they obey their father and mother and love God not because of rules, or fear, but because it has been engrained in them to live this way. Whether it's an example of an ancient family or a modern one, fathers are still impacting their children for good.

There is a heartrending story that is played out in too many homes today: It is that of a busy father and a son and/or daughter who longs to spend time with him. Fathers (and even some mothers) are missing out on many of the milestones in their children's lives because they are either out of town or simply too busy with the cares of life. They give their children toys, but never join in the fun; putting off until tomorrow what they need to do today – spend time with their child. There is a principle found in scripture that "...whatsoever a man soweth, that shall he also reap" (Galatians 6:7). This principle applies to the way we train up our children. If you are an absentee father you will train up an absentee child. Once you have slowed down enough to want to spend time with your child, they will be of an age that is too busy for you and later too busy for their own son or daughter. Is this the legacy you are working on? Or are you working toward the legacy of raising a son who will know how to call on God in times of trouble? Are you raising a daughter who will seek a man who will cherish her or mistreat her? Are you taking the time now to train up your child, or are you waiting for a more opportune time? Your child will only take that first step once. There is a precious short time to hear them say "Dada" as only a baby is able. Time goes quickly when they think you are the biggest, strongest, smartest dad around. We are not promised tomorrow; but if it does come, there is no promise it will make up for what is lost in the present.

Let's look again at Ephesians 6:4 (NLT): "Fathers, do not provoke your children to anger by the way you treat them." If fathers are our earthly example of our Heavenly Father, then their behavior is going to affect how their children view God. How will they be able to receive your instruction if you provoke your children to anger by taunting or teasing? How can they come to you with their hurts or mistakes if they are afraid of being belittled? Are your children going to want to approach you with their needs if they are afraid of being ridiculed or berated? How will they receive instruction from you if they are afraid they aren't good enough? They might begin to wonder how they could ever please the Lord if they are unable to please their daddy. If you provoke your children to anger by mistreating your wife, their mother, will they view God as a god who loves women or who mistreats them? If you provoke your children to anger by your absence from their life, then why would they expect God to show up when they need Him? Even with God's infinite power and ability to again destroy the world from sin as He did with the flood, He chose instead to take our place and die a horrible, slow, painful, bloody death so we can be forgiven and live for eternity with him. Fathers, how can you model this loving, merciful God to your children? You can model Christ's love by telling your children to come to you and take them up in your arms as He did (Matthew 10:14, 16). Then they will be ready to receive "the discipline and instruction that comes from the Lord."

I am blessed to have a husband that understands the importance of being an intentional father. Each morning before my husband goes off to work he takes the time to say goodbye to our girls along with a hug and a kiss. They love being adored by their daddy! They also see their daddy's love toward their mommy by the way he treats me. Each morning he brings me coffee (that I've prepared the night before to brew in the morning) and we have a sweet time together sharing our thoughts, dreams, and what we are studying in the Word. Our girls know we have this time together and they love to come in our room and say good morning, get some love, then begin their day. They also hear their daddy say things like, "Thank you for dinner," (even if it wasn't one of my best meals). His actions are showing them what a loving father and husband looks like. If we had sons, he would be teaching them how to be a godly husband as well as how to be a father someday. On the occasion when my husband does have to "instruct" our girls, they are able to receive it because they are confident in his love for them.

Fathers, you, too, can make a difference in your children whether yours by blood or adoption. You have the God ordained honor to be the head of your home, the father of your children and train them up in the way they should go. You are your child's earthly example of their Heavenly Father:

> You parents—if your children ask for a loaf of bread, do you give them a stone instead? Or if they ask for a fish, do you give them a snake? Of course not! So if you sinful people know how to give good gifts to your children, how much more will your heavenly

Father give good gifts to those who ask him? Matthew 7:9-11 (NLT)

Are you giving them good gifts: gifts of provision, protection, strength, counsel, guidance, encouragement, wisdom, love, compassion, and comfort? By exhibiting these things, you are their example of a wonderful, loving, powerful, providing God who is their everlasting Father! And by being this example God can tell your child, "Walk as your father walked."

Tips to help:

- Draw near to God and he will draw near to you.
- Set aside time each day to spend with your Father so you can cover your family in prayer.
- Take time to read books, like <u>Bringing up Boys</u> by Dr. James Dobson if you have a son, or <u>She Calls Me Daddy</u> by Robert Wolgemuth if you have a daughter. These are just two of many books written that can help you be the daddy you are called to be.
- Take time to play with your kids. It doesn't matter the age, become a kid again yourself and play ball! Play chess! Go fishing! Just take your child with you, one at a time or all at once. Have fun being a father!
- Lead your family in worship of the Lord.

Prayer: Heavenly Father, how can I best represent you? I want my children to see you when they look at me. I want them to know that just as I would do anything for them, you love us in the same way. Help me to model how much you love the church by how I love their mother. Help me also teach them that though I am not perfect, you are; when I make a mistake, I have to answer to you just as they answer to their mother and me. Help me to be the priest of our home and lead them in worship of you. Help me to leave behind footprints that glorify you. Thank you everlasting Father for the honor you have bestowed upon me to be a father to your child. In the name of our Heavenly Father, Jesus, Amen.

Chapter 9

Discipline
Proverbs 19:18

Discipline your children while there is hope. Otherwise you will ruin their lives.

Discipline: A word that causes angst in every parent and child. Parents dislike implementing it, and children dislike receiving any form of it. But as intentional parents we must also follow the Lord's example in discipline:

> For the LORD disciplines those he loves, and he punishes each one he accepts as his child." As you endure this divine discipline, remember that God is treating you as his own children. Who ever heard of a child who is never disciplined by its father? If God doesn't discipline you as he does all of his children, it means

that you are illegitimate and are not really his children at all. Hebrews 12: 6-8 (NLT)

In Hebrews, it is assumed that as a parent you are disciplining your child because you love them. How else could God inspire Paul to use this analogy, a quote from Proverbs 3:11-12, to help us understand how the Lord disciplines us? "My child, don't reject the LORD's discipline, and don't be upset when he corrects you. For the LORD corrects those he loves, just as a father corrects a child in whom he delights."

It is very plain to see, that if you love your child, you are expected as an intentional parent to discipline them. If your child understands you, as their parent, love them and discipline them, then they'll understand God is showing love when He "punishes" His children. I know I've been chastened by the Lord before, and it doesn't feel too good; but I know it's for my own good. I know this because I had loving parents who corrected me when I did wrong, and I learned what that felt like.

A father has the amazing ability to give the "look." A child sees the *look* and responds, knowing that the *look* means they are about to get it. That "it" is not a pleasant thing to the child hence the *look* is enough to strike fear in their very being. That is why discipline is so important; it puts a healthy fear in them toward sinning. Sin has consequences and the consequences should not be pleasant:

Fear of the LORD is the foundation of true knowledge, but fools despise wisdom and discipline. Proverbs 1:7 (NLT)

Fear of the LORD is the foundation of wisdom. Knowledge of the Holy One results in good judgment. Proverbs 9:10 (NLT)

Fear of the LORD teaches wisdom; humility precedes honor. Proverbs 15:33 (NLT)

True humility and fear of the LORD lead to riches, honor, and long life. Proverbs 22: 4 (NLT)

Fathers, as your child's earthly example of their Heavenly Father, you help them understand what the "fear of the Lord" is. It is to respect and be in awe of His authority. If the fear of the Lord is the beginning of wisdom and the foundation of knowledge, then it is important for our children to understand what it is. They must respect God and who He is if they are to have good judgment, riches, honor, and a long life. "Those who spare the rod of discipline hate their children. Those who love their children care enough to discipline them" (Proverbs 13:24 NLT).

If your child is about to touch a hot stove do you stand idly by waiting for them to get burned? No, unless you hate them. A loving parent, rushes over saying "NO!" intercepting at the last moment a little hand and a hot burner. If your toddler is walking out into a busy street, do you stand idly by watching to see if the cars will stop? No, unless you hate them. A loving parent leaps to grab their hand and again tells them, "Stop!" or "No!" and holds on so they will learn not to walk out into a street. If you ask your three year-old to hand you what he's playing with and, instead, he hides it behind his back and says he doesn't have it do you think it's cute? No, unless you hate them. A loving parent says, "Do not lie, show me your hands." If your teen-age child is caught stealing, would you make excuses for them and blame a materialistic society? Only if you hate them. A loving parent makes them pay the consequences.

We are by nature, sinners, we don't teach our children to sin, that comes naturally, what we teach them is to sin not. "A youngster's heart is filled with foolishness, but physical discipline will drive it far away" (Proverbs 22:15 NLT). When your children are very young, you discipline them to help them understand things can hurt them, or they can hurt something in their environment. Once they reach about three, they understand right from wrong, as illustrated in a three year old hiding something and lying about it. Now they have to be disciplined for sinning. As they grow older they become more skilled at figuring out how to skirt the law. This is why children must be intentionally parented and tied to Jesus. You must discipline them "while there is hope."

Parent, it's not good enough to expect them to know they shouldn't sin. They have to understand there are not only consequences for sin while on earth, but there are also eternal consequences. If you don't discipline your children, you "hate" them;

you don't care enough for their soul to teach them that obedience to God's commands is imperative. If they are tied to Jesus and know the Truth, sinning won't be so appealing and obedience will be easier. In our fallen nature, obedience does not come naturally; yet, according to 1 Samuel 15:22, obedience is greater than sacrifice. This is a lesson I have continually taught my girls. King Saul lost his kingship and all rights to the throne because of his disobedience!

When our girls were still very young, I thought counting to three, and giving them a chance to obey, was the way to do it. Much to my chagrin, my husband helped me understand this was not the way to handle disobedience. I thought I was being kind and loving by giving them all these chances. I was not looking at it as I hated them; yet, each time they didn't obey, I was allowing them to sin without an immediate consequence. Inadvertently, I was teaching them, that it's okay to sin a few times, but after that, well, then you're in trouble! What my husband said that finally made sense to me was, "If they are about to walk out into the street and could be run over, are you going to give them three chances to obey?" It was a bit extreme, but it made sense. By the count of two, they would be dead. In the same way, if we wait too long to expect obedience from our children, they could be dead spiritually. We can't allow them to get away with things while young because it's *cute* and then, when they get a little older and it's no longer thought cute, expect them to easily give up that behavior. It's much easier to nip things in the bud than have to cut off a whole branch.

There are different methods to discipline, and one of them must be "the rod." Scripture says, "Don't fail to discipline your children. They won't die if you spank them. Physical discipline may well save them from death" (Proverbs 23:13-14 NLT). Those are strong and wise words. Spanking your child should never be enjoyed. I don't believe God enjoys "spanking" us, but He understands it will get our attention and help us turn from our wicked ways. When I became a parent I turned to a trusted expert on parenting, Dr. Dobson. I purchased his parenting books and they blessed and empowered me as a mommy. One thing he encourages is to use something other than your hand to spank with. Our hand should be used to show love and comfort not as a tool to inflict pain. Spanking should also be done in love, not anger.

Many parents say they are scared of the way they feel when they are frustrated with their children, and are afraid of harming them. Before I began expecting immediate obedience and following up with immediate consequences, I, too, would be exasperated that they would not obey. That they hadn't obeyed, even after all those chances, would make me angry. But once I took control, by explaining the behavior expected and the consequence that would come if not obeyed the first time, I no longer got frustrated with my child. I followed through in my terms not theirs. I became the adult, and they had to play by my rules. This took away the pressure of having to figure out how to handle bad behavior while in a frustrated state of mind.

When discussing the rod, as referred to in scripture, it is important to keep in mind it was a tool used by shepherds. The rod was not used to harm the sheep; it was used to protect them. If a sheep begins to stray, the shepherd can expertly toss the rod at it to get its attention and call it back to the fold. A shepherd is willing to die protecting his sheep. This kind of love is not going to use the rod for injury, but for protection from the sheep's own tendency to wander off from safety. Sin separates us from God (Isaiah 59:2) and when we are separated from Him, He cannot protect us. This is when God has to "spank" us! In this same manner, there are times when the rod is needed to get our children's attention to make sure they stay protected.

"To discipline a child produces wisdom, but a mother is disgraced by an undisciplined child" (Proverbs 29:15 NLT). We've all heard "spare the rod, spoil the child." While that is not an actual scripture, it is based on the ones I have listed in this chapter. I want to address how sparing the rod spoils a child. Have you ever seen a child (another parent's child of course!) that you would say is "spoiled?" Usually they are known by their trademark whine, use of the word NO, and overall disrespect and disobedience. Why are they spoiled? Because they have not been disciplined.

Have you ever smelled a rotten potato? Let's call it a spoiled rotten potato. It's not very pleasant is it? How about spoiled meat? Rotting fish? How about rotting food in a dumpster? These are not pleasant aromas. They do not make you want to linger nearby enjoying their fragrance. This is how a spoiled child is. They stink to those who suffer their behavior. When my daughters have rotten attitudes, I tell them they stink! I even act like I'm smelling them. This may sound mean, or perhaps funny, but it gets the point across. They want to be a sweet smelling aroma to our home and their Lord. So, by saying this I bring attention to their behavior and give them the opportunity to correct it. This may not work so well with boys, who try to be smelly, but to girls this is simply unacceptable! I hope you hear my humor. Disciplining can be fun when you get creative and personalize it to your children's needs. There is not a one-size fits all method. Each child's willpower is different and will require more or less "punishment" from you. Some children respond merely to the "look" while others require the "rod." If you are being an intentional parent, and training up your child in the Way he should go, then you will have the Lord's help in the process of disciplining your child.

While my girls were early elementary age, my husband and I decided that we would not punish our girls if they had done wrong and confessed it. We wanted there to be incentive to tell the truth, as apposed to them being inclined to lie out of fear of punishment. These kinds of wrongs are different from direct defiance or disobedience to your authority. I'm talking about things like; "Mommy, I threw my ball in the living room and broke the lamp." This does not mean there is not a consequence; we just don't discipline them in the same way as if they lied and were caught. There is always a consequence for bad choices. In the case of breaking something, they may have to clean it up or pay for it, depending on what it was and how it happened. The key here is that they are glad they confessed. Because of this rule they have felt safe to tell us some interesting things, and we are thankful they feel free to do this. Just as God deals kindly with those who freely confess their sins, so do we.

As our children grow older it is necessary to modify our methods of discipline. What worked when they were young children does not work when they are twelve or sixteen. The hope is that the discipline they received while younger will help guide them when older. However, there will still be times that you have to do some pruning. For the older child it may be taking away friend time, video games, or phone privileges. Whatever it is that will "hurt" if you take it away. The idea is reinforcing that there are still consequences for wrong choices and you still have the authority to enforce the punishment. Just because your child may be as tall as you, it doesn't mean they are an adult. Teens are every bit as self-centered as toddlers so the attitudes you are dealing with are actually much the same. You are just dealing with a toddler who is bigger and can now express their feeling with words. So, don't be intimidated by your teen. They are still your child and should still honor you as such. When they are toddlers and they reach out to stick their finger in an electrical outlet you quickly pull their hand back. When they are teens and want to reach for inappropriate things you need to be just as quick! It is impossible to live in this world and avoid all temptations. What we can do is make sure our children are equipped with the Word to know how to recognize and handle these temptations. If they give in to the temptation we must be prepared to discipline them in love.

I have made it a point to share with my daughters some of the temptations that they will face as they get older. I want them to be prepared for it and see it for what it is. I think it is wise for our children to know the enemy so they aren't blind-sided by his tactics. For example, when my daughter first hinted at the attitude "I'm almost a teen so mom is now my enemy," I explained to her, "The enemy would love nothing more than to put a wedge between us so that you won't respect or listen to me any longer. If this takes place he knows that you won't listen to me and I can no longer protect you." I made her think on the truth, the fact that her mommy and daddy love her very much and do everything to protect her and provide for her. Why then would I be the enemy. As I stated earlier, teens tend to be self-centered. Because of this they will think we are trying to keep them from what they want rather than the truth that we are protecting them from what could be harmful. If these attitudes are allowed to develop you will lose your ability to train your child. You wouldn't leave a big ugly caterpillar to chomp on your prize winning vine. Why then would you allow ugly attitudes to remain in your child who you want to win the ultimate prize?

"Discipline your children, and they will give you peace of mind and will make your heart glad"

(Proverbs 29:17 NLT). I can say that now that my girls are tweens, they are beginning to respond out of wanting to do the right thing, not out of fear of what will happen if they don't. This is how I know Proverbs 29:17 is true. Are my children "perfect"? No, and neither are their parents. But I do see them growing in the fear of the Lord, and this makes my heart glad and gives me peace of mind.

Tips to help:

- Be consistent in your discipline. Don't confuse your child by requiring one thing today and another tomorrow.
- Be the adult. It's okay to expect their compliance with your rules.
- Purchase a book such as <u>Creative Corrections</u> by Lisa Whelchel. The title explains it.
- Ask the Lord for help. He can deal with matters of the heart that we can't seem to reach.

Prayer: Father, I thank you for loving me enough to correct me when I do wrong. Help me as I show the same love to my child. I want to train your child to respect you and obey your Word. Help me to be consistent in my expectations and in the consequences I require for bad choices. In everything we do we are to give you glory, even in disciplining our children. Thank you for your Word that teaches us and guides us in all things. In Jesus name I pray, Amen.

Chapter 10

Lost and Found
Luke 15:24

*For this my son was dead, and is alive again;
he was lost, and is found.*

Does the story of the Prodigal Son nullify the principles that have been taught in this book? No. Remember, our children are not naturally a vine that clings to Jesus; but if "trained," when they do make a mistake and stray away, they will know "The Way" back.

One of the great mysteries of parenting is how parents can seemingly raise all their children the same way, and yet they all turn out differently. Of course, remembering that they are God's creations and each one is unique helps us understand why each is so different. What worked on one child may not work for another, and what we do with our first-born is usually quite different from the last. This is why it is vital that God is at the center of your intentional parenting. We are limited in our knowledge, but God knows all things. We can only see the outward manifestations of what is in our child's heart, but God actually knows what's in it! So we have to include Him in our homes as their Heavenly Father, the third parent if you will permit me to say:

> Likewise, two people lying close together can keep each other warm. But how can one be warm alone? A person standing alone can be attacked and defeated, but two can stand back-to-back and conquer. Three are even better, for a triple-braided cord is not easily broken. Ecclesiastes 4:11-12 (NLT)

If you are a single parent, remember, you are not alone if you have God in your life. He will stand back-to-back with you ready to conquer. For homes with a mother and father, you are "even better" if you include God in your marriage and parenting; this combination is not easily broken. Including God always makes us stronger.

Why some children seem more inclined to learn the hard way is not something I can answer. But for those who are parenting these children I say, make sure you are there to love them after they have learned their lesson.

In the parable of the prodigal, we see a modern family as well as an ancient one. I cannot create a story of wanting the world, repenting, grace, self-righteousness, and a loving father any better than the one already written, so let's look at Luke 15:11b-31 (NLT):

> Jesus told them this story: "A man had two sons. The younger son told his father, 'I want my share of your estate now before you die.' So his father agreed to divide his wealth between his sons. "A few days later this younger son packed all his belongings and moved to a distant land, and there he wasted all his money in wild living. About the time his money ran out, a great famine swept over the land, and he began to starve. He persuaded a local farmer to hire him, and the man sent him into his fields to feed the pigs. The young man became so hungry that even the pods he was feeding the pigs looked good to him. But no one gave him anything. "When he finally came to his senses, he said to himself, 'At home even the hired servants have food enough to spare, and here I am dying of hunger! I will go home to my father and say, "Father, I have sinned against both heaven and you, and I am no longer worthy of being called your son. Please take me on as a hired servant."'" "So he returned home to his father. And while he was still a long way off, his father saw him coming. Filled with love and compassion, he ran to his son, embraced him, and kissed him. His son said to him, 'Father, I have sinned against both heaven and you, and I am no longer worthy

of being called your son. "But his father said to the servants, 'Quick! Bring the finest robe in the house and put it on him. Get a ring for his finger and sandals for his feet. And kill the calf we have been fattening. We must celebrate with a feast, for this son of mine was dead and has now returned to life. He was lost, but now he is found.' So the party began. "Meanwhile, the older son was in the fields working. When he returned home, he heard music and dancing in the house, and he asked one of the servants what was going on. 'Your brother is back,' he was told, 'and your father has killed the fattened calf. We are celebrating because of his safe return.' "The older brother was angry and wouldn't go in. His father came out and begged him, but he replied, 'All these years I've slaved for you and never once refused to do a single thing you told me to. And in all that time you never gave me even one young goat for a feast with my friends. Yet when this son of yours comes back after squandering your money on prostitutes, you celebrate by killing the fattened calf!' "His father said to him, 'Look, dear son, you have always stayed by me, and everything I have is yours."

Throughout this book, my desire has been to show, that in the Word of God, we have examples of the kind of parents God wants us to be. In this story, we first see a son who is itching to spread his wings.

We don't know that he had been a foolish son or that he had not been a hard worker before he asked for his inheritance. What we know is that when he asked his father if he could go, the father let him. This parent recognized there was something in his son that thought what the world had to offer was better than the life he was raised in. Now that this child was an adult what had been instilled in him would have to be his guide. The father let him go.

This child did not just move down the street, but went to a distant land; most likely where no one knew him, his family, or his God. In this place he wasted all the money his father had given him. Then, as he was getting down to his last penny, a famine hit and his penny couldn't even buy food! He began to starve and so sought out a job. No doubt leaning upon skills he had learned growing up, he persuaded a farmer into hiring him. The farmer sent him out to feed the pigs, and he was so desperate he was willing to eat what the pigs ate!

I just love this story!! The hand of God is so apparent in all that came his way. Here is a child of God, who no doubt had a father back home praying for him. Because of this, God was making sure he learned what exactly the world had to offer. He had his fun, his time of enjoying sin for a season; but when reality set in, the principles that were within him kicked in. Suddenly responsibility didn't look so bad, and because he had been taught to work, he got a job. God, with His wonderful sense of humor made sure his job was one that would humble him and remind him how far he had come and how deep he had sunk.

Here is this child who had led a good life, a blessed life, but thought he needed to taste the world. He tasted it all right! He tasted the same stuff the pigs ate; and as a Jew, he had been forbidden not only from eating pigs but feeding them as well. God knows how to reach each one of us in a very personal way. By allowing this child to be in this situation, the Lord was able to remind him where he had come from. The scripture says he came to his senses. The lie that satan had tempted him with, the lie that sin is great and he was missing out, suddenly disappeared. The Truth that he had been taught as a boy set him free! The Truth that he had been tied to conquered the lie that he had believed.

Now that he understands what he has done, he knows what he must do. Repent! We know he was truly repentant because he wasn't looking for someone else to blame, or excuses to tell his father; he was ready to confess, to admit he was wrong and accept the consequences.

It says when he was still a long way off his father saw him. This is not a picture of a father that disinherited his son after his son turned his back on his upbringing. This is a picture of a loving father waiting every day for the promise that if he trained his child up in the way he should go, when he is old he will not depart from it.

Jesus used parables that his audience could relate to. Perhaps this parable was not just a story. Perhaps there was a father in the crowd fretting about his son whom he loved, and Jesus told this parable not only to show His love for His people, but to assure this father, "your son will come home." Perhaps this is why in the story the father saw him while still afar off. Could it be that Jesus' words helped the father *see* his son coming home, even before he came? I like to think so.

If you have a prodigal child, I urge you to continue steadfastly in prayer for that child. Their Heavenly Father hears your prayers and will make a way to reach your child in a personal way. A way that will speak to them where they're at, whether it's a palace or a pig's sty. Watch for your child to return to you and be ready to run to meet them.

I don't want to overlook the end of this story; the lesson of the older brother. We must be careful that while we watch and wait for the prodigal, we don't ignore the children who remain faithful. The brother in this story becomes offended at the show of love and attention given to his brother who had gone out and squandered his father's money. Now, I'm not sure he was really bothered by the fact that it had been his father's money as much as the fact that he had worked so hard to be good and didn't get rewarded for it, while his wasteful brother did! At first glance, I have to agree; my human reasoning says "it's not fair." But what he didn't take into account was how great a father's love is, and he was buying into the lie that he was himself perfect. Whenever we begin to think we are perfect, we are going to get bitter about others who we think are sinners getting blessed! We don't choose to live a righteous life because of the rewards we will receive on this earth; we choose living a righteous life because it brings glory to our Father, and we will be rewarded an eternity with Him. It is important for us to teach our children we don't do good so we can be lifted up and treated as something special; we do good because it is the right thing to do. The older brother needed to understand he already had all that was his father's. He needed to understand his brother's waywardness was not being celebrated, his return was. We have to be careful we don't let a spirit of self-righteousness creep in to our children's lives when they choose the right path. Our children need to understand no one is perfect and none is without sin (Romans 3:10, 23). This will help them not get puffed up in their own eyes and judge others.

Through this parable, Jesus teaches how a parent should treat their wayward child. It is the same way our Heavenly Father treats us when we go astray. It is unconditional love. The father didn't wait for the child to beg and plead for forgiveness. He didn't wait to love him based on whether or not he learned his lesson; instead he tells his servants to celebrate the return of his lost son! He let his child know, "I know you've made a mistake, but more importantly I know you have come home. You remembered what I taught you and you made a choice to return to the God of your fathers, so I rejoice! You were dead, but are now alive; you were lost but now are found! I love you no matter what!"

Intentional parenting: Training up our children in the Way they should go so when they are old, they will not depart from it. Remembering where the Lord has brought us from, so we don't forget and fall back into sin. Becoming as a child that we might diligently teach our children the Word of God and model for them a life lived unto God. Teaching our children they are a child of God, and He has plans for their life. Becoming the parent God wants us to be.

Prayer: Thank you Jesus for dying for us that we might not die! Thank you for loving us in spite of our faults and failings. Thank you for loving us unconditionally. Thank you for teaching me through this parable how I should love my children if they should ever walk away. Thank you for grace and mercy. Thank you for love that forgives and rejoices in though I was lost, now I am found. I know that my child is always safe in your loving arms and you can reach them wherever they may go. Your love knows no bounds. In your loving and compassionate name Jesus, Amen!

CPSIA information can be obtained at www.ICGtesting.com
228417LV00001B/13/P